MznLnx

Missing Links Exam Preps

Exam Prep for

Advanced Modern Algebra

Rotman, 1st Edition

The MznLnx Exam Prep is your link from the texbook and lecture to your exams.
The MznLnx Exam Preps are unauthorized and comprehensive reviews of your textbooks.

All material provided by MznLnx and Rico Publications (c) 2010
Textbook publishers and textbook authors do not particpate in or contribute to these reviews.

MznLnx

Rico
Publications

Exam Prep for Advanced Modern Algebra
1st Edition
Rotman

Publisher: Raymond Houge
Assistant Editor: Michael Rouger
Text and Cover Designer: Lisa Buckner
Marketing Manager: Sara Swagger
Project Manager, Editorial Production: Jerry Emerson
Art Director: Vernon Lowerui

Product Manager: Dave Mason
Editorial Assitant: Rachel Guzmanji
Pedagogy: Debra Long
Cover Image: Jim Reed/Getty Images
Text and Cover Printer: City Printing, Inc.
Compositor: Media Mix, Inc.

(c) 2010 Rico Publications
ALL RIGHTS RESERVED. No part of this work covered by the copyright may be reproduced or used in any form or by an means--graphic, electronic, or mechanical, including photocopying, recording, taping, Web distribution, information storage, and retrieval systems, or in any other manner--without the written permission of the publisher.

Printed in the United States
ISBN:

For more information about our products, contact us at:
Dave.Mason@RicoPublications.com

For permission to use material from this text or product, submit a request online to:
Dave.Mason@RicoPublications.com

Contents

CHAPTER 1
Things Past — 1

CHAPTER 2
Groups I — 11

CHAPTER 3
Commutative Rings I — 25

CHAPTER 4
Fields — 43

CHAPTER 5
Groups II — 49

CHAPTER 6
Commutative Rings II — 57

CHAPTER 7
Modules and Categories — 73

CHAPTER 8
Algebras — 84

CHAPTER 9
Advanced Linear Algebra — 101

CHAPTER 10
Homology — 124

CHAPTER 11
Commutative Rings III — 132

ANSWER KEY — 146

TO THE STUDENT

COMPREHENSIVE

The *MznLnx* Exam Prep series is designed to help you pass your exams. Editors at MznLnx review your textbooks and then prepare these practice exams to help you master the textbook material. Unlike study guides, workbooks, and practice tests provided by the texbook publisher and textbook authors, *MznLnx* gives you **all** of the material in each chapter in exam form, not just samples, so you can be sure to nail your exam.

MECHANICAL

The MznLnx Exam Prep series creates exams that will help you learn the subject matter as well as test you on your understanding. Each question is designed to help you master the concept. Just working through the exams, you gain an understanding of the subject--its a simple mechanical process that produces success.

INTEGRATED STUDY GUIDE AND REVIEW

MznLnx is not just a set of exams designed to test you, its also a comprehensive review of the subject content. Each exam question is also a review of the concept, making sure that you will get the answer correct without having to go to other sources of material. You learn as you go! Its the easiest way to pass an exam.

HUMOR

Studying can be tedious and dry. MznLnx's instructional design includes moderate humor within the exam questions on occassion, to break the tedium and revitalize the brain

Chapter 1. Things Past

1. In mathematics, especially in the area of abstract algebra known as ring theory, a _____ is a ring with 0 ≠ 1 such that ab = 0 implies that either a = 0 or b = 0 (the zero-product property.) That is, it is a nontrivial ring without left or right zero divisors. A commutative _____ is called an integral _____.
   - a. Partially-ordered ring
   - b. Coherent ring
   - c. Subring
   - d. Domain

2. The _____ are natural numbers including 0 ' href='/wiki/0_(number)'>0, 1, 2, 3, ...) and their negatives (0, −1, −2, −3, ...). They are numbers that can be written without a fractional or decimal component, and fall within the set {...
   - a. ADE classification
   - b. Integers
   - c. Abelian P-root group
   - d. AKS primality test

3. In mathematics, especially in elementary arithmetic, _____ is an arithmetic operation which is the inverse of multiplication.

Specifically, if c times b equals a, written:

$$c \times b = a$$

where b is not zero, then a divided by b equals c, written:

$$\frac{a}{b} = c$$

For instance,

$$\frac{6}{3} = 2$$

since

$$2 \times 3 = 6.$$

In the above expression, a is called the dividend, b the divisor and c the quotient.

   - a. -module
   - b. 2-bridge knot
   - c. -equivalence
   - d. Division

4. In algebraic geometry, divisors are a generalization of codimension one subvarieties of algebraic varieties; two different generalizations are in common use, Cartier divisors and Weil divisors The concepts agree on non-singular varieties over algebraically closed fields.

A Weil _____ is a locally finite linear combination (with integral coefficients) of irreducible subvarieties of codimension one.

a. Lefschetz pencil
b. Linear system of divisors
c. Picard group
d. Divisor

5. In mathematics, an _____ is an isomorphism from a mathematical object to itself. It is, in some sense, a symmetry of the object, and a way of mapping the object to itself while preserving all of its structure. The set of all automorphisms of an object forms a group, called the _____ group.

a. Automorphism
b. Endomorphism
c. ADE classification
d. Epimorphism

6. In abstract algebra, a _____ is an algebraic structure with notions of addition, subtraction, multiplication and division, satisfying certain axioms. The most commonly used fields are the _____ of real numbers, the _____ of complex numbers, and the _____ of rational numbers, but there are also finite fields, fields of functions, various algebraic number fields, p-adic fields, and so forth.

Any _____ may be used as the scalars for a vector space, which is the standard general context for linear algebra.

a. Generic polynomial
b. Separable
c. Tensor product of fields
d. Field

7. In mathematics, _____ or factoring is the decomposition of an object ' href='/wiki/Matrix_(mathematics)'>matrix) into a product of other objects, or factors, which when multiplied together give the original. For example, the number 15 factors into primes as 3 × 5, and the polynomial $x^2 - 4$ factors as $(x - 2)(x + 2)$. In all cases, a product of simpler objects is obtained.

a. -equivalence
b. -module
c. 2-bridge knot
d. Factorization

8. In mathematics, a _____ is, roughly speaking, a commutative ring in which every element, with special exceptions, can be uniquely written as a product of prime elements, analogous to the fundamental theorem of arithmetic for the integers. Unique factorization domains are sometimes called factorial rings, following the terminology of Bourbaki.

Note that unique factorization domains appear in the following chain of class inclusions:

- Commutative rings ⊃ integral domains ⊃ unique factorization domains ⊃ principal ideal domains ⊃ Euclidean domains ⊃ fields

a. Isomorphism class
b. Unit ring
c. Absorption law
d. Unique factorization domain

9. The _____ is a result about congruences in number theory and its generalizations in abstract algebra.

The original form of the theorem, contained in a third-century AD book Sun Zi suanjing by Chinese mathematician Sun Tzu and later republished in a 1247 book by Qin Jiushao, the Shushu Jiuzhang (æ•¸æ›¸ä¹ ç« Mathematical Treatise in Nine Sections) is a statement about simultaneous congruences

Suppose $n_1, n_2, \ldots, n_k$ are positive integers which are pairwise coprime.

    a. Chinese remainder theorem   b. Discrete logarithm
    c. Modular arithmetic   d. Multiplicative group of integers modulo n

10. In ring theory, a branch of abstract algebra, an _____ is a special subset of a ring. The _____ concept generalizes in an appropriate way some important properties of integers like 'even number' or 'multiple of 3'.

For instance, in rings one studies prime ideals instead of prime numbers, one defines coprime ideals as a generalization of coprime numbers, and one can prove a generalized Chinese remainder theorem about ideals.

    a. ADE classification   b. Augmentation ideal
    c. AKS primality test   d. Ideal

11. In ring theory, a branch of abstract algebra, a _____ is an ideal I in a ring R that is generated by a single element a of R.

More specifically:

- a left _____ of R is a subset of R of the form $Ra := \{ra : r \text{ in } R\}$;
- a right _____ is a subset of the form $aR := \{ar : r \text{ in } R\}$;
- a two-sided _____ is a subset of the form $RaR := \{r_1 a s_1 + \ldots + r_n a s_n : r_1, s_1, \ldots, r_n, s_n \text{ in } R\}$.

If R is a commutative ring, then the above three notions are all the same. In that case, it is common to write the ideal generated by a as (a.)

Not all ideals are principal.

    a. Radical of an ideal   b. Radical of an ring
    c. Primitive ideal   d. Principal ideal

12. In abstract algebra, a _____ i.e., can be generated by a single element. More generally, a principal ring is a nonzero commutative ring whose ideals are principal, although some authors (e.g., Bourbaki) refers to Principal ideal domains as principal rings. The distinction being that a principal ideal ring may have zero divisors whereas a _____ cannot.

    a. Discrete valuation   b. Minimal prime
    c. Nilradical   d. Principal ideal domain

13. In linear algebra, a _____ is a set of vectors that, in a linear combination, can represent every vector in a given vector space or free module, and such that no element of the set can be represented as a linear combination of the others. In other words, a _____ is a linearly independent spanning set.

    a. Basis   b. Minor
    c. Chirality   d. Supergroup

14. In mathematics, the complex numbers are an extension of the real numbers obtained by adjoining an imaginary unit, denoted i, which satisfies:

$$i^2 = -1.$$

Every _____ can be written in the form a + bi, where a and b are real numbers called the real part and the imaginary part of the _____, respectively.

Complex numbers are a field, and thus have addition, subtraction, multiplication, and division operations. These operations extend the corresponding operations on real numbers, although with a number of additional elegant and useful properties, e.g., negative real numbers can be obtained by squaring complex (imaginary) numbers.

   a. -module
   c. 2-bridge knot
   b. -equivalence
   d. Complex number

15. In mathematics, in the field of algebraic number theory, a _____ is a formal product of places of an algebraic number field. It is used to encode ramification data for abelian extensions of number field.

Let K be an algebraic number field with ring of integers R. A _____ is a formal product

$$\mathbf{m} = \prod_{\mathbf{p}} \mathbf{p}^{\nu(\mathbf{p})}$$

where p runs over all places of K, finite or infinite, the exponents v are zero except for finitely many p, for real places r we have v (r)=0 or 1 and for complex places v=0.

   a. Different ideal
   c. Principal ideal theorem
   b. Quadratic field
   d. Modulus

16. In mathematics, particularly in linear algebra and functional analysis, the _____ of a matrix or linear operator is a factorization analogous to the polar form of a nonzero complex number z

$$z = re^{i\theta}$$

where r is the absolute value of z (a positive real number), and $e^{i\theta}$ is called the complex sign of z.

The _____ of a complex matrix A is a matrix decomposition of the form

$$A = UP$$

where U is a unitary matrix and P is a positive-semidefinite Hermitian matrix. This decomposition always exists; and so long as A is invertible, it is unique, with P positive-definite.

Chapter 1. Things Past

a. Riesz-Thorin theorem
b. Cholesky decomposition
c. Positive definite function on a group
d. Polar decomposition

17. _____ is the mathematical process of putting things together. The plus sign '+' means that numbers are added together. For example, in the picture on the right, there are 3 + 2 apples--meaning three apples and two other apples--which is the same as five apples, since 3 + 2 = 5.

a. ADE classification
b. AKS primality test
c. Abelian P-root group
d. Addition

18. In mathematics, an _____ is a formula such as that for the exponential function

$$e^{x+y} = e^x \cdot e^y$$

that expresses, for a particular function f, f(x + y) in terms of f(x) and f(y.) Slightly more generally, as is the case with the trigonometric functions sin and cos, several functions may be involved; this is more apparent than real, in that case, since there cos is an algebraic function of sin (in other words, we usually take their functions both as defined on the unit circle.)

The scope of the idea of an _____ was fully explored in the nineteenth century, prompted by the discovery of the _____ for elliptic functions.

a. Algebraic stack
b. Arithmetic group
c. Algebraic cycle
d. Addition theorem

19. The _____ and descending chain condition (DCC) are finiteness properties satisfied by certain algebraic structures, most importantly, ideals in a commutative ring. These conditions played an important role in the development of the structure theory of commutative rings in the works of David Hilbert, Emmy Noether, and Emil Artin. The conditions themselves can be stated in an abstract form, so that they make sense for any partially ordered set.

a. Atomic domain
b. Invariant polynomial
c. Ascending chain condition
d. Integral

20. In algebraic topology, a simplicial k-_____ is a formal linear combination of k-simplices.

Integration is defined on chains by taking the linear combination of integrals over the simplices in the _____ with coefficients typically integers. The set of all k-chains forms a group and the sequence of these groups is called a _____ complex.

a. Tesseract
b. Combinatorial topology
c. Bockstein homomorphism
d. Chain

21. In mathematics, a _____ of a number x is any number which, when repeatedly multiplied by itself, eventually yields x:

$$r \times r \times \cdots \times r = x.$$

In terms of exponentiation, r is a _____ of x if

$$r^n = x$$

for some positive integer n. For example, 2 is a _____ of 16 since $2^4 = 2 \times 2 \times 2 \times 2 = 16$.

The number n is called the degree of the _____.

- a. Rationalisation
- b. Difference of two squares
- c. Cubic function
- d. Root

22. An nth _____, where n = 1,2,3,···, is a complex number, z, satisfying the equation

$$z^n = 1.$$

Second roots are called square roots, and third roots are called cube roots.

An nth _____ is primitive if

$$z^k \neq 1 \quad (k = 1, 2, 3, \ldots, n-1).$$

There are n different nth roots of unity:

$$z^k \quad (k = 1, 2, 3, \ldots, n),$$

where z is any primitive nth _____. These n roots are distributed evenly over the unit circle as can be seen in the plot on the right-hand side of the three 3rd roots of unity.

- a. 2-bridge knot
- b. -module
- c. -equivalence
- d. Root of unity

23. In algebra, the nth _____, for any positive integer n, is the monic polynomial

where the product is over all primitive n^{th} roots of unity ω, i.e. all the complex numbers ω of order n.

The degree of Φ_n, or in other words the number of factors in its definition above, is φ(n), where φ is Euler's totient function.

The coefficients of Φ_n are integers.

a. Cyclic number
b. Q-Vandermonde identity
c. Character group
d. Cyclotomic polynomial

24. In mathematics, a _____ is a constant multiplicative factor of a certain object. For example, in the expression $9x^2$, the _____ of x^2 is 9.

The object can be such things as a variable, a vector, a function, etc.

a. Coefficient
b. Constant term
c. Vandermonde polynomial
d. Tschirnhaus transformation

25. In algebra, a _____ of an element in a quadratic extension field of a field K is its image under the unique non-identity automorphism of the extended field that fixes K. If the extension is generated by a square root of an element r of K, then the _____ of $a + b\sqrt{r}$ is $a - b\sqrt{r}$ for $a, b \in K$, and in particular in the case of the field C of complex numbers as an extension of the field R of real numbers (where r = − 1), the complex _____ of a + bi is a − bi.

Forming the sum or product of any element of the extension field with its _____ always gives an element of K. This can be used to rewrite a quotient of numbers in the extended field so that the denominator lies in K, by multiplying numerator and denominator by the _____ of the denominator. This process is called rationalization of the denominator, in particular if K is the field Q of rational numbers.

a. Field arithmetic
b. K-theory
c. Digital root
d. Conjugate

26. In mathematics, a _____ is the direct product of two sets. The _____ is named after René Descartes, whose formulation of analytic geometry gave rise to this concept.

Specifically, the _____ of two sets X (for example the points on an x-axis) and Y (for example the points on a y-axis), denoted X × Y, is the set of all possible ordered pairs whose first component is a member of X and whose second component is a member of Y (e.g. the whole of the x-y plane):

$$X \times Y = \{(x,y) | x \in X \text{ and } y \in Y\}.$$

For example, the _____ of the 13-element set of standard playing card ranks {Ace, King, Queen, Jack, 10, 9, 8, 7, 6, 5, 4, 3, 2} and the four-element set of card suits {â™ , â™¥, â™¦, â™£} is the 52-element set of all possible playing cards {(Ace, â™), (King, â™), ..., (2, â™), (Ace, â™¥), ..., (3, â™£), (2, â™£)}.

a. Cartesian product
b. -module
c. Pointed set
d. -equivalence

27. In mathematics, a _____ is an algebraic structure whose main use is in studying geometric objects such as Lie groups and differentiable manifolds. Lie algebras were introduced to study the concept of infinitesimal transformations. The term '_____') was introduced by Hermann Weyl in the 1930s.

a. Weyl group
c. Lorentz group
b. Maximal torus
d. Lie algebra

28. A _____ is a set G closed under a binary operation · satisfying the following 3 axioms:

- Associativity: For all a, b and c in G, (a · b) · c = a · (b · c.)
- Identity element: There exists an e∈G such that for all a in G, e · a = a · e = a.
- Inverse element: For each a in G, there is an element b in G such that a · b = b · a = e, where e is an identity element.

Basic examples for groups are the integers Z with addition operation, or rational numbers without zero Q{0} with multiplication. More generally, for any ring R, the units in R form a multiplicative _____ Groups include, however, much more general structures than the above.

a. Product of group subsets
c. Grigorchuk group
b. Group
d. Nilpotent group

29. In mathematics, given two groups (G, *) and (H, Â·), a _____ from (G, *) to (H, Â·) is a function h : G → H such that for all u and v in G it holds that

$$h(u * v) = h(u) \cdot h(v)$$

where the group operation on the left hand side of the equation is that of G and on the right hand side that of H.

From this property, one can deduce that h maps the identity element e_G of G to the identity element e_H of H, and it also maps inverses to inverses in the sense that

$h(u^{-1}) = h(u)^{-1}$.

Hence one can say that h 'is compatible with the group structure'.

Older notations for the homomorphism h(x) may be x_h, though this may be confused as an index or a general subscript.

a. Pair
c. Baby-step giant-step
b. Metanilpotent group
d. Group homomorphism

30. A _____ between two algebras over a field K, A and B, is a map $F : A \to B$ such that for all k in K and x,y in A,

- F(kx) = kF(x)

- F(x + y) = F(x) + F(y)

- F(xy) = F(x)F(y)

If F is bijective then F is said to be an isomorphism between A and B.

Let A = K[x] be the set of all polynomials over a field K and B be the set of all polynomial functions over K. Both A and B are algebras over K given by the standard multiplication and addition of polynomials and functions, respectively. We can map each f in A to $\hat{f}$ in B by the rule $\hat{f}(t) = f(t)$. A routine check shows that the mapping $f \mapsto \hat{f}$ is a _____ of the algebras A and B. If K is a finite field then let

$$p(x) = \Pi_{t \in K}(x - t).$$

p is a nonzero polynomial in K[x], however $p(t) = 0$ for all t in K, so $\hat{p} = 0$ is the zero function and the algebras are not isomorphic.

a. Tensor product of algebras
b. Frobenius matrix
c. Tensor algebra
d. Homomorphism

31. In mathematics and group theory, a _____ system for the action of a group G on a set X is a partition of X that is G-invariant. In terms of the associated equivalence relation on X, G-invariance means that

x ≡ y implies gx ≡ gy

for all g in G and all x, y in X. The action of G on X determines a natural action of G on any _____ system for X.

Each element of the _____ system is called a _____.

a. Frobenius group
b. Parker vector
c. Symmetric group
d. Block

32. In abstract algebra, the concept of a _____ over a ring is a generalization of the notion of vector space, where instead of requiring the scalars to lie in a field, the 'scalars' may lie in an arbitrary ring. Modules also generalize the notion of abelian groups, which are modules over $\mathbb{Z}$.

Thus, a _____, like a vector space, is an additive abelian group; a product is defined between elements of the ring and elements of the _____, and this multiplication is associative (when used with the multiplication in the ring) and distributive.

a. Semigroupoid
c. Near-field

b. Goodman-Nguyen-van Fraassen algebra
d. Module

Chapter 2. Groups I

1. In several fields of mathematics the term _____ is used with different but closely related meanings. They all relate to the notion of mapping the elements of a set to other elements of the same set, i.e., exchanging (or 'permuting') elements of a set.

The general concept of _____ can be defined more formally in different contexts:

In combinatorics, a _____ is usually understood to be a sequence containing each element from a finite set once, and only once.

   a. Near-field
   c. Rupture field
   b. Permutation
   d. Binary function

2. The set of all symmetry operations considered, on all objects in a set X, can be modeled as a group action g : G × X → X, where the image of g in G and x in X is written as g·x. If, for some g, g·x = y then x and y are said to be symmetrical to each other. For each object x, operations g for which g·x = x form a group, the _____ of the object, a subgroup of G. If the _____ of x is the trivial group then x is said to be asymmetric, otherwise symmetric.
   a. Symmetry group
   c. 2-bridge knot
   b. -equivalence
   d. -module

3. In mathematics, a _____ is an algebraic structure whose main use is in studying geometric objects such as Lie groups and differentiable manifolds. Lie algebras were introduced to study the concept of infinitesimal transformations. The term '_____') was introduced by Hermann Weyl in the 1930s.
   a. Maximal torus
   c. Weyl group
   b. Lorentz group
   d. Lie algebra

4. In mathematics, and in particular in group theory, a _____ is a permutation of the elements of some set X which maps the elements of some subset S to each other in a cyclic fashion, while fixing (i.e., mapping to themselves) all other elements. The set S is called the orbit of the _____.

A permutation of a set X, which is a bijective function $\sigma : X \rightarrow X$, is called a _____ if the action on X of the subgroup generated by σ has exactly one orbit with more than a single element.

   a. Nested radical
   c. Definition .
   b. Continuant
   d. Cycle

5. In abstract algebra, the _____ of a module is a measure of the module's 'size'. It is defined as the _____ of the longest ascending chain of submodules and is a generalization of the concept of dimension for vector spaces. The modules with finite _____ share many important properties with finite-dimensional vector spaces.
   a. Finitely generated module
   c. Supermodule
   b. Morita equivalence
   d. Length

6. In abstract algebra, the concept of a _____ over a ring is a generalization of the notion of vector space, where instead of requiring the scalars to lie in a field, the 'scalars' may lie in an arbitrary ring. Modules also generalize the notion of abelian groups, which are modules over $\mathbb{Z}$.

Chapter 2. Groups I

Thus, a _____, like a vector space, is an additive abelian group; a product is defined between elements of the ring and elements of the _____, and this multiplication is associative (when used with the multiplication in the ring) and distributive.

- a. Module
- b. Goodman-Nguyen-van Fraassen algebra
- c. Near-field
- d. Semigroupoid

7. In informal language, a _____ is a function that swaps two elements of a set. More formally, given a finite set $X = \{a_1, a_2, \ldots, a_n\}$, a _____ is a permutation (bijective function of X onto itself) f, such that there exist indices i,j such that $f(a_i) = a_j$, $f(a_j) = a_i$ and $f(a_k) = a_k$ for all other indices k. This is often denoted (in the cycle notation) as (a,b.)

For example, if X = {a,b,c,d,e}, the function σ given by

$$\sigma(a) = a$$
$$\sigma(b) = e$$
$$\sigma(c) = c$$
$$\sigma(d) = d$$
$$\sigma(e) = b$$

is a _____.

Any permutation can be expressed as the composition (product) of transpositions.

- a. Transposition
- b. Cycle notation
- c. Rencontres number
- d. Stirling numbers of the first kind

8. In mathematics, especially in the area of abstract algebra known as ring theory, a _____ is a ring with 0 ≠ 1 such that ab = 0 implies that either a = 0 or b = 0 (the zero-product property.) That is, it is a nontrivial ring without left or right zero divisors. A commutative _____ is called an integral _____.

- a. Subring
- b. Coherent ring
- c. Domain
- d. Partially-ordered ring

9. In mathematics, _____ or factoring is the decomposition of an object ' href='/wiki/Matrix_(mathematics)'>matrix) into a product of other objects, or factors, which when multiplied together give the original. For example, the number 15 factors into primes as 3 × 5, and the polynomial $x^2 - 4$ factors as (x − 2)(x + 2.) In all cases, a product of simpler objects is obtained.

- a. Factorization
- b. 2-bridge knot
- c. -equivalence
- d. -module

10. In mathematics, a _____ is, roughly speaking, a commutative ring in which every element, with special exceptions, can be uniquely written as a product of prime elements, analogous to the fundamental theorem of arithmetic for the integers. Unique factorization domains are sometimes called factorial rings, following the terminology of Bourbaki.

Chapter 2. Groups I

Note that unique factorization domains appear in the following chain of class inclusions:

- Commutative rings $\supsetneq$ integral domains $\supsetneq$ unique factorization domains $\supsetneq$ principal ideal domains $\supsetneq$ Euclidean domains $\supsetneq$ fields

a. Unit ring
c. Unique factorization domain
b. Isomorphism class
d. Absorption law

11. In mathematics, a _____ is any function which can be written as the ratio of two polynomial functions. _____ of degree 2 : $y = \dfrac{x^2 - 3x - 2}{x^2 - 4}$

In the case of one variable, x, a _____ is a function of the form

$$f(x) = \frac{P(x)}{Q(x)}$$

where P and Q are polynomial function in x and Q is not the zero polynomial. The domain of f is the set of all points x for which the denominator Q(x) is not zero.

a. Legendre rational functions
c. -equivalence
b. -module
d. Rational function

12. In mathematics, the _____ of a ring R, often denoted char(R), is defined to be the smallest number of times one must add the ring's multiplicative identity element (1) to itself to get the additive identity element (0); the ring is said to have _____ zero if this repeated sum never reaches the additive identity. That is, char(R) is the smallest positive number n such that

$$\underbrace{1 + \cdots + 1}_{n \text{ summands}} = 0$$

if such a number n exists, and 0 otherwise. The _____ may also be taken to be the exponent of the ring's additive group, that is, the smallest positive n such that

$$\underbrace{a + \cdots + a}_{n \text{ summands}} = 0$$

for every element a of the ring (again, if n exists; otherwise zero.)

a. Coherent ring
c. Free ideal ring
b. Hereditary
d. Characteristic

Chapter 2. Groups I

13. In mathematics, _____ is a property that a binary operation can have. It means that, within an expression containing two or more of the same associative operators in a row, the order that the operations are performed does not matter as long as the sequence of the operands is not changed. That is, rearranging the parentheses in such an expression will not change its value.

   a. External
   b. Associativity
   c. Anticommutativity
   d. Identity element

14. A _____ is a set G closed under a binary operation · satisfying the following 3 axioms:

   - Associativity: For all a, b and c in G, (a · b) · c = a · (b · c.)
   - Identity element: There exists an e∈G such that for all a in G, e · a = a · e = a.
   - Inverse element: For each a in G, there is an element b in G such that a · b = b · a = e, where e is an identity element.

Basic examples for groups are the integers Z with addition operation, or rational numbers without zero Q{0} with multiplication. More generally, for any ring R, the units in R form a multiplicative _____ Groups include, however, much more general structures than the above.

   a. Grigorchuk group
   b. Group
   c. Product of group subsets
   d. Nilpotent group

15. In its simplest meaning in mathematics and logic, an _____ is an action or procedure which produces a new value from one or more input values. There are two common types of operations: unary and binary. Unary operations involve only one value, such as negation and trigonometric functions.

   a. Abelian P-root group
   b. AKS primality test
   c. ADE classification
   d. Operation

16. An _____ is a group satisfying the requirement that the result of applying the group operation to two group elements does not depend on their order Abelian groups generalize the arithmetic of addition of integers; they are named after Niels Henrik Abel.

The concept of an _____ is one of the first concepts encountered in undergraduate abstract algebra, with many other basic objects, such as a module and a vector space, being its refinements.

   a. ADE classification
   b. Algebraically compact
   c. Elementary abelian group
   d. Abelian group

17. The _____ is a result about congruences in number theory and its generalizations in abstract algebra.

The original form of the theorem, contained in a third-century AD book Sun Zi suanjing by Chinese mathematician Sun Tzu and later republished in a 1247 book by Qin Jiushao, the Shushu Jiuzhang (æ•¸æ›¸ä¹ ç« Mathematical Treatise in Nine Sections) is a statement about simultaneous congruences

Suppose n_1, n_2, â€¦, n_k are positive integers which are pairwise coprime.

a. Discrete logarithm
b. Modular arithmetic
c. Multiplicative group of integers modulo n
d. Chinese remainder theorem

18. In mathematics, the _____, denoted by T (or in blackboard bold by $\mathbb{T}$), is the multiplicative group of all complex numbers with absolute value 1, i.e., the unit circle in the complex plane.

$$\mathbb{T} = \{z \in \mathbb{C} : |z| = 1\}.$$

The _____ forms a subgroup of $\mathbb{C}^\times$, the multiplicative group of all nonzero complex numbers. Since $\mathbb{C}^\times$ is abelian, it follows that T is as well.

a. Principal homogeneous space
b. Group object
c. Power automorphism
d. Circle group

19. In mathematics, the _____ of degree n is the set of n×n invertible matrices, together with the operation of ordinary matrix multiplication. This forms a group, because the product of two invertible matrices is again invertible, and the inverse of an invertible matrix is invertible. The name is because the columns of an invertible matrix are linearly independent, hence the vectors/points they define are in general linear position, and matrices in the _____ take points in general linear position to points in general linear position.

a. Linearly independent
b. Direct product
c. Valuation ring
d. General linear group

20. In mathematics, a _____ is a rectangular array of numbers. This way, matrices can record data that depend on multiple parameters. In particular they are used to keep track of the coefficients of multiple linear equations. Matrices are closely connected to linear transformations, which are higher-dimensional analogs of linear functions, i.e., functions of the form f(x) = c · x, where c is a constant. This map corresponds to a _____ with one row and column, with entry c. In addition to a number of elementary, entrywise operations such as _____ addition a key notion is _____ multiplication, which displays a number of features not encountered in numbers; for example, products of matrices depend on the order of the factors, unlike products of real numbers, say, where c · d = d · c for any two numbers c and d.

a. Commutativity
b. Polynomial expression
c. Heap
d. Matrix

21. If $A_1, A_2, ..., A_n$ are _____ square matrices over a field, then

$$(A_1 A_2 \cdots A_n)^{-1} = A_n^{-1} A_{n-1}^{-1} \cdots A_1^{-1}.$$

It becomes evident why this is the case if one attempts to find an inverse for the product of the A_is from first principles, that is, that we wish to determine B such that

$$(A_1 A_2 \cdots A_n) B = I$$

where B is the inverse matrix of the product. To remove A_1 from the product, we can then write

$$A_1^{-1}(A_1 A_2 \cdots A_n)B = A_1^{-1}I$$

which would reduce the equation to

$$(A_2 A_3 \cdots A_n)B = A_1^{-1}I.$$

Likewise, then, from

$$A_2^{-1}(A_2 A_3 \cdots A_n)B = A_2^{-1}A_1^{-1}I$$

which simplifies to

$$(A_3 A_4 \cdots A_n)B = A_2^{-1}A_1^{-1}I.$$

If one repeat the process up to A_n, the equation becomes

$$B = A_n^{-1}A_{n-1}^{-1} \cdots A_2^{-1}A_1^{-1}I$$

$$B = A_n^{-1}A_{n-1}^{-1} \cdots A_2^{-1}A_1^{-1}$$

but B is the inverse matrix, i.e. $B = (A_1 A_2 \cdots A_n)^{-1}$ so the property is established.

Over the field of real numbers, the set of singular n-by-n matrices, considered as a subset of $R^{n \times n}$, is a null set, i.e., has Lebesgue measure zero.

    a. 2-bridge knot   b. Nonsingular
    c. -equivalence   d. -module

22. In linear algebra, a _____ is a set of vectors that, in a linear combination, can represent every vector in a given vector space or free module, and such that no element of the set can be represented as a linear combination of the others. In other words, a _____ is a linearly independent spanning set.
    a. Basis   b. Chirality
    c. Minor   d. Supergroup

23. In group theory, a branch of mathematics, the term _____ is used in two closely related senses:

- the _____ of a group is its cardinality, i.e. the number of its elements;
- the _____, sometimes period, of an element a of a group is the smallest positive integer m such that a^m = e (where e denotes the identity element of the group, and a^m denotes the product of m copies of a.) If no such m exists, we say that a has infinite _____. All elements of finite groups have finite _____.

We denote the _____ of a group G by ord(G) or $|G|$ and the _____ of an element a by ord(a) or $|a|$.

Example. The symmetric group S_3 has the following multiplication table.

This group has six elements, so ord(S_3) = 6.

a. Index calculus algorithm
b. Outer automorphism group
c. Order
d. Artin group

24. In mathematics, a _____ is the group of symmetries of a regular polygon, including both rotations and reflections. Dihedral groups are among the simplest examples of finite groups, and they play an important role in group theory, geometry, and chemistry.

There are two competing notations for the _____ associated to a polygon with n sides.

a. Characteristic subgroup
b. Rank of a group
c. Group representations
d. Dihedral group

25. In mathematics, an _____ is the group of even permutations of a finite set. The _____ on the set {1,...,n} is called the _____ of degree n, or the _____ on n letters and denoted by A_n or Alt(n.)

For instance, the _____ of degree 4 is A_4 = {e, (123), (132), (124), (142), (134), (143), (234), (243), (12)(34), (13)(24), (14)(23)}

a. Extra special groups
b. Octahedral symmetry
c. Icosahedral symmetry
d. Alternating group

26. In group theory, a _____ is a group that can be generated by a single element, in the sense that the group has an element g (called a 'generator' of the group) such that, when written multiplicatively, every element of the group is a power of g (a multiple of g when the notation is additive.) The 6th complex roots of unity form a _____ under multiplication. ζ is a primitive element, but $ζ^2$ is not, because the odd powers of ζ are not a power of $ζ^2$.

A group G is called cyclic if there exists an element g in G such that G = <g> = { g^n | n is an integer }.

a. Cyclic group
b. Finitely generated abelian group
c. Locally cyclic group
d. Torsion subgroup

27. The _____ are natural numbers including 0 ' href='/wiki/0_(number)'>0, 1, 2, 3, ...) and their negatives (0, −1, −2, −3, ...). They are numbers that can be written without a fractional or decimal component, and fall within the set {...

a. AKS primality test
b. ADE classification
c. Abelian P-root group
d. Integers

28. A _____ is a left or right _____ of some subgroup in G. Since Hg = g‰(‰g⁻¹Hg‰), the right cosets Hg (of H‰) and the left cosets g‰(‰g⁻¹Hg‰) (of the conjugate subgroup g⁻¹Hg‰) are the same. Hence it is not meaningful to speak of a _____ as being left or right unless one first specifies the underlying subgroup.

For abelian groups or groups written additively, the notation used changes to g+H and H+g respectively.

a. Burnside ring
b. Wreath product
c. Coset
d. Grigorchuk group

29. In mathematics, specifically group theory, the _____ of a subgroup H in a group G is the e;relative sizee; of H in G. For example, if H has _____ 2 in G, then intuitively e;halfe; of the elements of G lie in H. The _____ of H in G is usually denoted |G : H| or [G : H].

If G and H are finite groups, then the _____ of H in G is simply the quotient of the orders of the two groups:

$$|G : H| = \frac{|G|}{|H|}.$$

By Lagrange's theorem, this number is always a positive integer.

If G and H are infinite, then the _____ of H is G is defined as the number of cosets of H in G.

a. Inner automorphism
b. Even permutations
c. Outer automorphism
d. Index

30. In mathematics, the _____ of degree n over a field F is the set of n×n matrices with determinant 1, with the group operations of ordinary matrix multiplication and matrix inversion. This is the normal subgroup of the general linear group, given by the kernel of the determinant

$$\det \colon \mathrm{GL}(n, F) \to F^\times.$$

where we write $F^\times$ for the multiplicative group of F (that is, excluding 0.)

These elements are 'special' in that they fall on a subvariety of the general linear group - they satisfy a polynomial equation (since the determinant is polynomial in the entries.)

a. Special linear group
c. Semiring
b. Simple
d. Zero divisor

31. A _____ between two algebras over a field K, A and B, is a map $F : A \to B$ such that for all k in K and x,y in A,

- F(kx) = kF(x)

- F(x + y) = F(x) + F(y)

- F(xy) = F(x)F(y)

If F is bijective then F is said to be an isomorphism between A and B.

Let A = K[x] be the set of all polynomials over a field K and B be the set of all polynomial functions over K. Both A and B are algebras over K given by the standard multiplication and addition of polynomials and functions, respectively. We can map each f in A to $\hat{f}$ in B by the rule $\hat{f}(t) = f(t)$. A routine check shows that the mapping $f \mapsto \hat{f}$ is a _____ of the algebras A and B. If K is a finite field then let

$$p(x) = \Pi_{t \in K}(x - t).$$

p is a nonzero polynomial in K[x], however $p(t) = 0$ for all t in K, so $\hat{p} = 0$ is the zero function and the algebras are not isomorphic.

a. Tensor algebra
c. Frobenius matrix
b. Tensor product of algebras
d. Homomorphism

32. In abstract algebra, an _____ is a bijective map f such that both f and its inverse f $^{-1}$ are homomorphisms, i.e., structure-preserving mappings. In the more general setting of category theory, an _____ is a morphism f:X→Y in a category for which there exists an 'inverse' f $^{-1}$:Y→X, with the property that both f $^{-1}$f=id$_X$ and ff $^{-1}$=id$_Y$.

Informally, an _____ is a kind of mapping between objects, which shows a relationship between two properties or operations.

a. Isomorphism
c. Endomorphism
b. Epimorphism
d. ADE classification

33. In mathematics, given two groups (G, *) and (H, Â·), a _____ from (G, *) to (H, Â·) is a function h : G → H such that for all u and v in G it holds that

$$h(u * v) = h(u) \cdot h(v)$$

where the group operation on the left hand side of the equation is that of G and on the right hand side that of H.

From this property, one can deduce that h maps the identity element e_G of G to the identity element e_H of H, and it also maps inverses to inverses in the sense that

$$h(u^{-1}) = h(u)^{-1}.$$

Hence one can say that h 'is compatible with the group structure'.

Older notations for the homomorphism h(x) may be x_h, though this may be confused as an index or a general subscript.

    a. Baby-step giant-step   b. Metanilpotent group
    c. Group homomorphism   d. Pair

34. In the various branches of mathematics that fall under the heading of abstract algebra, the _____ of a homomorphism measures the degree to which the homomorphism fails to be injective. An important special case is the _____ of a matrix, also called the null space.

The definition of _____ takes various forms in various contexts.

    a. Completing the square   b. Kernel
    c. K-theory   d. Monomial basis

35. In mathematics, more specifically in abstract algebra, a _____ is a special kind of subgroup. Normal subgroups are important because they can be used to construct quotient groups from a given group.

Évariste Galois was the first to realize the importance of the existence of normal subgroups.

    a. Hanna Neumann conjecture   b. Characteristic subgroup
    c. Cayley graph   d. Normal subgroup

36. In linear algebra, the _____ states that every square matrix over the real or complex field satisfies its own characteristic equation.

More precisely; if A is the given n×n matrix and I_n is the n×n identity matrix, then the characteristic polynomial of A is defined as:

where 'det' is the determinant function. The _____ states that substituting the matrix A in the characteristic polynomial (which involves multiplying its constant term by I_n, since that is the zeroth power of A) results in the zero matrix:

The _____ also holds for square matrices over commutative rings.

a. -module
b. Cayley-Hamilton theorem
c. -equivalence
d. 2-bridge knot

37. The term _____ or centre is used in various contexts in abstract algebra to denote the set of all those elements that commute with all other elements. More specifically:

- The _____ of a group G consists of all those elements x in G such that xg = gx for all g in G. This is a normal subgroup of G.
- The _____ of a ring R is the subset of R consisting of all those elements x of R such that xr = rx for all r in R. The _____ is a commutative subring of R, so R is an algebra over its _____.
- The _____ of an algebra A consists of all those elements x of A such that xa = ax for all a in A. See also: central simple algebra.
- The _____ of a Lie algebra L consists of all those elements x in L such that [x,a] = 0 for all a in L. This is an ideal of the Lie algebra L.
- The _____ of a monoidal category C consists of pairs (A,u) where A is an object of C, and $u : A \otimes - \to - \otimes A$ a natural isomorphism satisfying certain axioms.

a. Left alternative
b. Ring theory
c. Center
d. Self-adjoint

38. In mathematics, an _____ is an isomorphism from a mathematical object to itself. It is, in some sense, a symmetry of the object, and a way of mapping the object to itself while preserving all of its structure. The set of all automorphisms of an object forms a group, called the _____ group.

a. Epimorphism
b. Endomorphism
c. ADE classification
d. Automorphism

39. In abstract algebra, a _____ is an algebraic structure with notions of addition, subtraction, multiplication and division, satisfying certain axioms. The most commonly used fields are the _____ of real numbers, the _____ of complex numbers, and the _____ of rational numbers, but there are also finite fields, fields of functions, various algebraic number fields, p-adic fields, and so forth.

Any _____ may be used as the scalars for a vector space, which is the standard general context for linear algebra.

a. Tensor product of fields
b. Generic polynomial
c. Separable
d. Field

40. In abstract algebra, an _____ of a group G is a function

$$f : G \to G$$

defined by

$$f(x) = axa^{-1}, \text{ for all } x \text{ in } G,$$

where a is a given fixed element of G.

The operation axa^{-1} is called conjugation Informally, in a conjugation a certain operation is applied, then another one (x) is carried out, and then the initial operation is reversed.

a. Extensible automorphism
b. IA automorphism
c. Inner automorphism
d. Idempotent measure

41. _____, in mathematics, are a non-commutative number system that extends the complex numbers. The _____ were first described by Irish mathematician Sir William Rowan Hamilton in 1843 and applied to mechanics in three-dimensional space. They find uses in both theoretical and applied mathematics, in particular for calculations involving three-dimensional rotations , such as in 3D computer graphics, although they have been superseded in many applications by vectors and matrices.

a. Split-biquaternion
b. Generalized quaternion interpolation
c. Split-quaternions
d. Quaternions

42. In mathematics, specifically abstract algebra, the _____ are three theorems that describe the relationship between quotients, homomorphisms, and subobjects. Versions of the theorems exist for groups, rings, vector spaces, modules, Lie algebras, and various other algebraic structures. In universal algebra, the _____ can be generalized to the context of algebras and congruences.

a. Isomorphism theorems
b. Identity theorem for Riemann surfaces
c. ADE classification
d. AKS primality test

43. The _____ and descending chain condition (DCC) are finiteness properties satisfied by certain algebraic structures, most importantly, ideals in a commutative ring. These conditions played an important role in the development of the structure theory of commutative rings in the works of David Hilbert, Emmy Noether, and Emil Artin. The conditions themselves can be stated in an abstract form, so that they make sense for any partially ordered set.

a. Invariant polynomial
b. Atomic domain
c. Ascending chain condition
d. Integral

44. In algebraic topology, a simplicial k-_____ is a formal linear combination of k-simplices.

Integration is defined on chains by taking the linear combination of integrals over the simplices in the _____ with coefficients typically integers. The set of all k-chains forms a group and the sequence of these groups is called a _____ complex.

    a. Bockstein homomorphism   b. Combinatorial topology
    c. Chain   d. Tesseract

45. In algebra and geometry, a _____ is a way of describing symmetries of objects using groups. The essential elements of the object are described by a set and the symmetries of the object are described by the symmetry group of this set, which consists of bijective transformations of the set. In this case, the group is also called a permutation group (especially if the set is finite or not a vector space) or transformation group (especially if the set is a vector space and the group acts like linear transformations of the set.)

    a. Group action   b. Group
    c. Free group   d. Modular group

46. In group theory, the _____ and normalizer of a subset S of a group G are subgroups of G which have a restricted action on the elements of S and S as a whole, respectively. These subgroups provide insight into the structure of G.

The _____ of an element a of a group G (written as $C_G(a)$) is the set of elements of G which commute with a; in other words, $C_G(a) = \{x \in G : xa = ax\}$.

    a. Stallings' theorem about ends of groups   b. Centralizer
    c. Class automorphism   d. HN group

47. In mathematics, especially group theory, the elements of any group may be partitioned into conjugacy classes; members of the same _____ share many properties, and study of conjugacy classes of non-abelian groups reveals many important features of their structure. In all abelian groups every _____ is a set containing one element (singleton set.)

Functions that are constant for members of the same _____ are called class functions.

    a. Maximal subgroup   b. Homeomorphism group
    c. Group isomorphism problem   d. Conjugacy class

48. In algebra, a _____ of an element in a quadratic extension field of a field K is its image under the unique non-identity automorphism of the extended field that fixes K. If the extension is generated by a square root of an element r of K, then the _____ of $a + b\sqrt{r}$ is $a - b\sqrt{r}$ for $a, b \in K$, and in particular in the case of the field C of complex numbers as an extension of the field R of real numbers (where r = − 1), the complex _____ of a + bi is a − bi.

Forming the sum or product of any element of the extension field with its _____ always gives an element of K. This can be used to rewrite a quotient of numbers in the extended field so that the denominator lies in K, by multiplying numerator and denominator by the _____ of the denominator. This process is called rationalization of the denominator, in particular if K is the field Q of rational numbers.

Chapter 2. Groups I

a. K-theory
b. Field arithmetic
c. Digital root
d. Conjugate

49. The iterated wreath products of cyclic groups of order p are very important examples of _____. Denote the cyclic group of order p as W(1), and the wreath product of W(n) with W(1) as W(n+1.) Then W(n) is the Sylow p-subgroup of the symmetric group Sym(p^n.)

a. P-groups
b. Group representations
c. Polycyclic group
d. History of group theory

50. In mathematics, the term _____ is used to describe an algebraic structures which in some sense cannot be divided by a smaller structure of the same type. Put another way, an algebraic structure is _____ if the kernel of every homomorphism is either the whole structure or a single element. Some examples are:

- A group is called a _____ group if it does not contain a non-trivial proper normal subgroup.
- A ring is called a _____ ring if it does not contain a non-trivial two sided ideal.
- A module is called a _____ module if does not contain a non-trivial submodule.
- An algebra is called a _____ algebra if does not contain a non-trivial two sided ideal.

The general pattern is that the structure admits no non-trivial congruence relations.

a. Simple
b. Linear combinations
c. Polarization identity
d. Commutativity

Chapter 3. Commutative Rings I

1. In ring theory, a branch of abstract algebra, a _____ is a ring in which the multiplication operation is commutative. The study of commutative rings is called commutative algebra.

   Some specific kinds of commutative rings are given with the following chain of class inclusions:

   - commutative rings ⊃ integral domains ⊃ unique factorization domains ⊃ principal ideal domains ⊃ Euclidean domains ⊃ fields

   A ring is a set R equipped with two binary operations, i.e. operations that combine any two elements of the ring to a third. They are called addition and multiplication and commonly denoted by '+' and '·', e.g. a + b and a · b.

   a. Nilradical
   b. Differential calculus over commutative algebras
   c. Going up
   d. Commutative ring

2. In mathematics, a _____ is a type of algebraic structure. There is some variation among mathematicians as to exactly what properties a _____ is required to have, as described in detail below. However, commonly a _____ is defined as a set together with two binary operations (usually called addition and multiplication), where each operation combines two elements to form a third element.

   a. -equivalence
   b. -module
   c. Ring
   d. 2-bridge knot

3. A _____ is a complex number whose real and imaginary part are both integers. The Gaussian integers, with ordinary addition and multiplication of complex numbers, form an integral domain, usually written as Z[i]. This domain does not have a total ordering that respects arithmetic, since it contains imaginary numbers.

   a. Gaussian integer
   b. Kummer sum
   c. Quadratic Gauss sums
   d. Jacobi sum

4. The _____ are natural numbers including 0 ' href='/wiki/0_(number)'>0, 1, 2, 3, ...) and their negatives (0, −1, −2, −3, ...). They are numbers that can be written without a fractional or decimal component, and fall within the set {...

   a. Abelian P-root group
   b. Integers
   c. ADE classification
   d. AKS primality test

5. In elementary algebra, a _____ is a polynomial with two terms--the sum of two monomials--often bound by parenthesis or brackets when operated upon. It is the simplest kind of polynomial other than monomials.

- The _____ $a^2 - b^2$ can be factored as the product of two other binomials:

    $a^2 - b^2 = (a + b)(a - b.)$

    This is a special case of the more general formula:

    $$a^{n+1} - b^{n+1} = (a-b)\sum_{k=0}^{n} a^k b^{n-k}$$

- The product of a pair of linear binomials (ax + b) and (cx + d) is:

    $(ax + b)(cx + d) = acx^2 + axd + bcx + bd.$

- A _____ raised to the nth power, represented as

    $(a + b)^n$

    can be expanded by means of the _____ theorem or, equivalently, using Pascal's triangle. Taking a simple example, the perfect square _____ $(p + q)^2$ can be found by squaring the first digit, adding twice the product of the first and second digit and finally adding the square of the second digit, to give $p^2 + 2pq + q^2$.

a. Content
b. Generalized arithmetic progression
c. Theory of equations
d. Binomial

6. In mathematics, the _____ is an important formula giving the expansion of powers of sums. Its simplest version states that

$$(x+y)^n = \sum_{k=0}^{n} \binom{n}{k} x^{n-k} y^k \qquad (1)$$

for any real or complex numbers x and y, and any non-negative integer n. The binomial coefficient appearing in (1) may be defined in terms of the factorial function n!:

$$\binom{n}{k} = \frac{n!}{k!\,(n-k)!}.$$

For example, here are the cases where 2 ≤ n ≤ 5:

$$(x+y)^2 = x^2 + 2xy + y^2$$
$$(x+y)^3 = x^3 + 3x^2y + 3xy^2 + y^3$$
$$(x+y)^4 = x^4 + 4x^3y + 6x^2y^2 + 4xy^3 + y^4$$
$$(x+y)^5 = x^5 + 5x^4y + 10x^3y^2 + 10x^2y^3 + 5xy^4 + y^5.$$

Formula (1) is valid more generally for any elements x and y of a semiring as long as xy = yx.

    a. -equivalence
    b. -module
    c. 2-bridge knot
    d. Binomial theorem

7. In ring theory, a branch of mathematics, a _____ is a rng (a ring without unity) in which the product of any two elements is 0 (the additive neutral element.)

A _____ is commutative, and every subring is an ideal.

Each abelian group can be turned into a _____ by defining the product of any two elements to be 0.

    a. Noetherian ring
    b. Zero ring
    c. Semiprime ring
    d. Witt vector

8. In mathematics, especially in the area of abstract algebra known as ring theory, a _____ is a ring with $0 \neq 1$ such that ab = 0 implies that either a = 0 or b = 0 (the zero-product property.) That is, it is a nontrivial ring without left or right zero divisors. A commutative _____ is called an integral _____.
    a. Subring
    b. Domain
    c. Partially-ordered ring
    d. Coherent ring

9. In mathematics, a _____ is a subset of a ring, which contains the multiplicative identity and is itself a ring under the same binary operations. Naturally, those authors who do not require rings to contain a multiplicative identity do not require subrings to possess the identity (if it exists.) This leads to the added advantage that ideals become subrings
    a. Kurosh problem
    b. Poisson ring
    c. Semiperfect ring
    d. Subring

10. In its simplest meaning in mathematics and logic, an _____ is an action or procedure which produces a new value from one or more input values. There are two common types of operations: unary and binary. Unary operations involve only one value, such as negation and trigonometric functions.
    a. AKS primality test
    b. Operation
    c. Abelian P-root group
    d. ADE classification

11. In mathematics, _____ or factoring is the decomposition of an object ' href='/wiki/Matrix_(mathematics)'>matrix) into a product of other objects, or factors, which when multiplied together give the original. For example, the number 15 factors into primes as 3 × 5, and the polynomial $x^2 - 4$ factors as (x − 2)(x + 2.) In all cases, a product of simpler objects is obtained.
    a. 2-bridge knot
    b. -equivalence
    c. -module
    d. Factorization

12. In mathematics, a _____ is, roughly speaking, a commutative ring in which every element, with special exceptions, can be uniquely written as a product of prime elements, analogous to the fundamental theorem of arithmetic for the integers. Unique factorization domains are sometimes called factorial rings, following the terminology of Bourbaki.

Note that unique factorization domains appear in the following chain of class inclusions:

- Commutative rings $\supset$ integral domains $\supset$ unique factorization domains $\supset$ principal ideal domains $\supset$ Euclidean domains $\supset$ fields

a. Unique factorization domain
b. Unit ring
c. Absorption law
d. Isomorphism class

13. In mathematics, a _____ in a (unital) ring R is an invertible element of R, i.e. an element u such that there is a v in R with

uv = vu = 1_R, where 1_R is the multiplicative identity element.

That is, u is an invertible element of the multiplicative monoid of R. If $0 \neq 1$ in the ring, then 0 is not a _____.

Unfortunately, the term _____ is also used to refer to the identity element 1_R of the ring, in expressions like ring with a _____ or _____ ring, and also e.g. '_____' matrix.

a. Ascending chain condition on principal ideals
b. Ore condition
c. Ore extension
d. Unit

14. In mathematics, a _____ on a field k is a function

$$\nu : k \to \mathbb{Z} \cup \{\infty\}$$

satisfying the conditions

$$\nu(x \cdot y) = \nu(x) + \nu(y)$$
$$\nu(x + y) \geq \min\{\nu(x), \nu(y)\}$$
$$\nu(x) = \infty \iff x = 0$$

Note that often the trivial valuation which takes on only the values $0, \infty$ is explicitly excluded.

To every field with _____ v we can associate the subring

$$\mathcal{O}_k := \{x \in k \mid \nu(x) \geq 0\}$$

of k, which is a _____ ring.

- a. Commutative ring
- b. Nilradical
- c. Going up
- d. Discrete valuation

15. In abstract algebra, a _____ is a principal ideal domain (PID) with exactly one non-zero maximal ideal.

This means a _____ is an integral domain R which satisfies any one of the following equivalent conditions:

1. R is a local principal ideal domain, and not a field.
2. R is a valuation ring with a value group isomorphic to the integers under addition.
3. R is a local Dedekind domain and not a field.
4. R is a noetherian local ring with Krull dimension one, and the maximal ideal of R is principal.
5. R is an integrally closed noetherian local ring with Krull dimension one.
6. R is a unique factorization domain with a unique irreducible element (up to multiplication with units.)
7. R is local, not a field, and every nonzero fractional ideal of R is irreducible.
8. There is some Dedekind valuation v on the field of fractions K of R, such that R={x : x in K, v(x) ≥ 0}.

Let $Z_{(2)}$={ p/q : p, q in Z, q odd }. Then the field of fractions of $Z_{(2)}$ is Q. Now, for any nonzero element r of Q, we can apply unique factorization to the numerator and denominator of r to write r as $2^k p/q$, where p, q, and k are integers with p and q odd. In this case, we define v(r)=k.

- a. Localization of a category
- b. Localization of a module
- c. Discrete valuation ring
- d. Localized

16. In abstract algebra, a _____ is an algebraic structure with notions of addition, subtraction, multiplication and division, satisfying certain axioms. The most commonly used fields are the _____ of real numbers, the _____ of complex numbers, and the _____ of rational numbers, but there are also finite fields, fields of functions, various algebraic number fields, p-adic fields, and so forth.

Any _____ may be used as the scalars for a vector space, which is the standard general context for linear algebra.

- a. Separable
- b. Tensor product of fields
- c. Field
- d. Generic polynomial

17. A _____ is a set G closed under a binary operation · satisfying the following 3 axioms:

- Associativity: For all a, b and c in G, (a · b) · c = a · (b · c.)
- Identity element: There exists an e∈G such that for all a in G, e · a = a · e = a.
- Inverse element: For each a in G, there is an element b in G such that a · b = b · a = e, where e is an identity element.

Chapter 3. Commutative Rings I

Basic examples for groups are the integers Z with addition operation, or rational numbers without zero Q{0} with multiplication. More generally, for any ring R, the units in R form a multiplicative _____ Groups include, however, much more general structures than the above.

- a. Group
- b. Grigorchuk group
- c. Product of group subsets
- d. Nilpotent group

18. In algebra (in particular in algebraic geometry or algebraic number theory), a _____ is a function on a field that provides a measure of size or multiplicity of elements of the field. They generalize to commutative algebra the notion of size inherent in consideration of the degree of a pole or multiplicity of a zero in complex analysis, the degree divisibility of a number by a prime number in number theory, and the geometrical concept of contact between two algebraic or analytic varieties in algebraic geometry.

A field with a _____ on it is called a valued field.

- a. Pencil
- b. Motivic integration
- c. Stable vector bundle
- d. Valuation

19. In abstract algebra, a _____ is an integral domain D such that for every element x of its field of fractions F, at least one of x or x^{-1} belongs to D.

Given a field F, if D is a subring of F such that either x or x^{-1} belongs to D for every x in F, then D is said to be a _____ for the field F. Since F is in this case indeed the field of fractions of D, a _____ for a field is a _____. Another way to characterize the valuation rings of a field F is that valuation rings D of F have F as their field of fractions, and their ideals are totally ordered by inclusion; or equivalently their principal ideals are totally ordered by inclusion.

- a. Left alternative
- b. Rupture field
- c. Near-field
- d. Valuation ring

20. In mathematics, a _____ R is a ring (with identity) for which $x^2 = x$ for all x in R; that is, R consists only of idempotent elements.

Boolean rings are automatically commutative and of characteristic 2 A _____ is essentially the same thing as a Boolean algebra, with ring multiplication corresponding to conjunction or meet ∧, and ring addition to exclusive disjunction or symmetric difference (not disjunction ∨.)

- a. Boolean ring
- b. Hereditary
- c. Ring of integers
- d. Domain

21. The _____ is a result about congruences in number theory and its generalizations in abstract algebra.

Chapter 3. Commutative Rings I

The original form of the theorem, contained in a third-century AD book Sun Zi suanjing by Chinese mathematician Sun Tzu and later republished in a 1247 book by Qin Jiushao, the Shushu Jiuzhang (æ•¸æ›¸ä¹ ç« Mathematical Treatise in Nine Sections) is a statement about simultaneous congruences

Suppose n_1, n_2, â€¦, n_k are positive integers which are pairwise coprime.

a. Multiplicative group of integers modulo n
b. Modular arithmetic
c. Chinese remainder theorem
d. Discrete logarithm

22. In mathematics, there are several meanings of _____ depending on the subject.

A _____, usually denoted by ° (the _____ symbol), is a measurement of plane angle, representing $1/360$ of a full rotation. When that angle is with respect to a reference meridian, it indicates a location along a great circle of a sphere, such as Earth, Mars, or the celestial sphere.

a. Degree
b. Median algebra
c. Relation algebra
d. Symmetric difference

23. In mathematics, a polynomial P(X) is _____ over a field K if all of its irreducible factors have distinct roots in an algebraic closure of K - that is each irreducible factor of P(X) has distinct linear factors in some large enough field extension. There is, however, another, non-equivalent definition of separability. It says that P is _____ if and only if it is coprime to its formal derivative P'.

a. Global field
b. Transcendence degree
c. Separable
d. Field of fractions

24. A _____ is a symbol that stands for a value that may vary; the term usually occurs in opposition to constant, which is a symbol for a non-varying value, i.e. completely fixed or fixed in the context of use. The concepts of constants and variables are fundamental to all modern mathematics, science, engineering, and computer programming.

Much of the basic theory for which we use variables today, such as school geometry and algebra, was developed thousands of years ago, but the use of symbolic formulae and variables is only several hundreds of years old.

a. -equivalence
b. -module
c. 2-bridge knot
d. Variable

25. In ring theory, a branch of abstract algebra, an _____ is a special subset of a ring. The _____ concept generalizes in an appropriate way some important properties of integers like 'even number' or 'multiple of 3'.

For instance, in rings one studies prime ideals instead of prime numbers, one defines coprime ideals as a generalization of coprime numbers, and one can prove a generalized Chinese remainder theorem about ideals.

a. ADE classification
b. AKS primality test
c. Augmentation ideal
d. Ideal

26. In mathematics, especially in the field of abstract algebra, a _____ is a ring formed from the set of polynomials in one or more variables with coefficients in another ring. Polynomial rings have influenced much of mathematics, from the Hilbert basis theorem, to the construction of splitting fields, and to the understanding of a linear operator. Many important conjectures, such as Serre's conjecture, have influenced the study of other rings, and have influenced even the definition of other rings, such as group rings and rings of formal power series.
   a. Nilradical
   b. Commutative ring
   c. Dedekind domain
   d. Polynomial ring

27. In ring theory, a branch of abstract algebra, a _____ is an ideal I in a ring R that is generated by a single element a of R.

More specifically:

- a left _____ of R is a subset of R of the form Ra := {ra : r in R};
- a right _____ is a subset of the form aR := {ar : r in R};
- a two-sided _____ is a subset of the form RaR := $\{r_1 a s_1 + ... + r_n a s_n : r_1, s_1, ..., r_n, s_n$ in R$\}$.

If R is a commutative ring, then the above three notions are all the same. In that case, it is common to write the ideal generated by a as (a.)

Not all ideals are principal.

   a. Primitive ideal
   b. Principal ideal
   c. Radical of an ideal
   d. Radical of an ring

28. In abstract algebra, a _____ i.e., can be generated by a single element. More generally, a principal ring is a nonzero commutative ring whose ideals are principal, although some authors (e.g., Bourbaki) refers to Principal ideal domains as principal rings. The distinction being that a principal ideal ring may have zero divisors whereas a _____ cannot.
   a. Nilradical
   b. Principal ideal domain
   c. Discrete valuation
   d. Minimal prime

29. In linear algebra, a _____ is a set of vectors that, in a linear combination, can represent every vector in a given vector space or free module, and such that no element of the set can be represented as a linear combination of the others. In other words, a _____ is a linearly independent spanning set.
   a. Basis
   b. Supergroup
   c. Minor
   d. Chirality

30. In mathematics, the _____ of a polynomial is the term of degree 0. For example, in the polynomial

$X^3 + 2X + 3$

over the variable X, the _____ is 3. Here, the _____ is given by a numeral, but it may also be specified by a letter that is a parameter rather than a variable, as in the polynomial

ax² + bx + c,

in the variable x, where a, b, and c are parameters so that c is the _____.

a. Constant term
b. Quadratic function
c. Characteristic polynomial
d. Symmetric polynomial

31. In mathematics, a _____ or quadratic is a polynomial of degree two. A _____ may involve a single variable x, or multiple variables such as x, y, and z.

Any single-variable _____ may be written as

$$ax^2 + bx + c,$$

where x is the variable, and a, b, and c represent the coefficients.

a. Sheffer sequence
b. Littlewood polynomial
c. Polynomial remainder theorem
d. Quadratic polynomial

32. _____ or biquadratic reciprocity is a collection of theorems in elementary and algebraic number theory that state conditions under which the congruence $x^4 \equiv p \pmod{q}$ is solvable; the word 'reciprocity' comes from the form of some of these theorems, in that they relate the solvability of the congruence $x^4 \equiv p \pmod{q}$ to that of $x^4 \equiv q \pmod{p}$.

Euler made the first conjectures about biquadratic reciprocity. Gauss published two monographs on biquadratic reciprocity.

a. Quartic
b. Cyclotomic character
c. Modulus
d. Herbrand quotient

33. In mathematics, a _____ is any function which can be written as the ratio of two polynomial functions. _____ of degree 2 :

$$y = \frac{x^2 - 3x - 2}{x^2 - 4}$$

In the case of one variable, x, a _____ is a function of the form

$$f(x) = \frac{P(x)}{Q(x)}$$

where P and Q are polynomial function in x and Q is not the zero polynomial. The domain of f is the set of all points x for which the denominator Q(x) is not zero.

  a. Rational function
  b. Legendre rational functions
  c. -module
  d. -equivalence

34. The _____ is often met for the first time as an operation on a single real function of a single real variable. One of the simplest settings for generalizations is to vector valued functions of several variables (most often the domain forms a vector space as well.) This is the field of multivariable calculus.
  a. Derivative
  b. -module
  c. -equivalence
  d. 2-bridge knot

35. In mathematics, _____ are devices that make it possible to employ much of the analytical machinery of power series in settings that do not have natural notions of convergence. They are also useful, especially in combinatorics, for providing compact representations of sequences and multisets, and for finding closed formulas for recursively defined sequences; this is known as the method of generating functions.

A _____ can be loosely thought of as a polynomial with infinitely many terms.

  a. Cokernel
  b. Matrix
  c. Multiplicative group
  d. Formal power series

36. In field theory, a branch of mathematics, a _____ of a finite field GF(q) is a generator of the multiplicative group of the field, which is necessarily cyclic. The minimal polynomial of a _____ is a primitive polynomial.
  a. Composite field
  b. Field of fractions
  c. Global field
  d. Primitive element

37. In mathematics, the adjective _____ means that an object cannot be expressed as a product of more than one non-trivial factors in a given set. See also factorization.

For any field F, the ring of polynomials with coefficients in F is denoted by F[x].

  a. Ehrhart polynomial
  b. Alternating polynomial
  c. Irreducible
  d. Integer-valued polynomial

38. In mathematics, a _____ of a number x is any number which, when repeatedly multiplied by itself, eventually yields x:

$$r \times r \times \cdots \times r = x.$$

In terms of exponentiation, r is a _____ of x if

$$r^n = x$$

for some positive integer n. For example, 2 is a _____ of 16 since $2^4 = 2 × 2 × 2 × 2 = 16$.

The number n is called the degree of the _____.

- a. Difference of two squares
- b. Cubic function
- c. Rationalisation
- d. Root

39. This article deals with the ring of complex numbers integral over Z. For the general notion of _____, see Integrality.

In number theory, an _____ is a complex number that is a root of some monic polynomial (leading coefficient 1) with coefficients in Z. The set of all algebraic integers is closed under addition and multiplication and therefore is a subring of complex numbers denoted by A. The ring A is the integral closure of regular integers Z in complex numbers.

The ring of integers of a number field K, denoted by O_K, is the intersection of K and A: it can also be characterised as the maximal order of the field K. Each _____ belongs to the ring of integers of some number field.

- a. Algebraic integer
- b. Additive polynomial
- c. Adele ring
- d. Algebraic number theory

40. In mathematics, the _____ of a ring R, often denoted char(R), is defined to be the smallest number of times one must add the ring's multiplicative identity element (1) to itself to get the additive identity element (0); the ring is said to have _____ zero if this repeated sum never reaches the additive identity. That is, char(R) is the smallest positive number n such that

$$\underbrace{1 + \cdots + 1}_{n \text{ summands}} = 0$$

if such a number n exists, and 0 otherwise. The _____ may also be taken to be the exponent of the ring's additive group, that is, the smallest positive n such that

$$\underbrace{a + \cdots + a}_{n \text{ summands}} = 0$$

for every element a of the ring (again, if n exists; otherwise zero.)

- a. Free ideal ring
- b. Coherent ring
- c. Hereditary
- d. Characteristic

41. A _____ between two algebras over a field K, A and B, is a map $F : A \to B$ such that for all k in K and x,y in A,

- F(kx) = kF(x)
- F(x + y) = F(x) + F(y)
- F(xy) = F(x)F(y)

If F is bijective then F is said to be an isomorphism between A and B.

Let A = K[x] be the set of all polynomials over a field K and B be the set of all polynomial functions over K. Both A and B are algebras over K given by the standard multiplication and addition of polynomials and functions, respectively. We can map each f in A to $\hat{f}$ in B by the rule $\hat{f}(t) = f(t)$. A routine check shows that the mapping $f \mapsto \hat{f}$ is a _____ of the algebras A and B. If K is a finite field then let

$$p(x) = \Pi_{t \in K}(x - t).$$

p is a nonzero polynomial in K[x], however $p(t) = 0$ for all t in K, so $\hat{p} = 0$ is the zero function and the algebras are not isomorphic.

a. Frobenius matrix
b. Tensor product of algebras
c. Tensor algebra
d. Homomorphism

42. In ring theory or abstract algebra, a _____ is a function between two rings which respects the operations of addition and multiplication.

More precisely, if R and S are rings, then a _____ is a function f : R → S such that

- f(a + b) = f(a) + f(b) for all a and b in R
- f(ab) = f(a) f(b) for all a and b in R
- f(1) = 1

Naturally, if one does not require rings to have a multiplicative identity then the last condition is dropped.

The composition of two ring homomorphisms is a _____. It follows that the class of all rings forms a category with ring homomorphisms as the morphisms (cf.

a. Global dimension
b. Group ring
c. Krull ring
d. Ring homomorphism

43. In mathematics, a _____ is an algebraic structure whose main use is in studying geometric objects such as Lie groups and differentiable manifolds. Lie algebras were introduced to study the concept of infinitesimal transformations. The term '_____') was introduced by Hermann Weyl in the 1930s.
   a. Weyl group
   b. Lorentz group
   c. Maximal torus
   d. Lie algebra

44. In mathematics, one can often define a _____ of objects already known, giving a new one. This is generally the Cartesian product of the underlying sets, together with a suitably defined structure on the product set. More abstractly, one talks about the product in category theory, which formalizes these notions.
   a. Precedence rule
   b. Special linear group
   c. Group extension
   d. Direct product

45. In abstract algebra, the concept of a _____ over a ring is a generalization of the notion of vector space, where instead of requiring the scalars to lie in a field, the 'scalars' may lie in an arbitrary ring. Modules also generalize the notion of abelian groups, which are modules over $\mathbb{Z}$.

Thus, a _____, like a vector space, is an additive abelian group; a product is defined between elements of the ring and elements of the _____, and this multiplication is associative (when used with the multiplication in the ring) and distributive.

   a. Goodman-Nguyen-van Fraassen algebra
   b. Near-field
   c. Module
   d. Semigroupoid

46. In geometry, a _____ is a quadrilateral with two sets of parallel sides. The opposite or facing sides of a _____ are of equal length, and the opposite angles of a _____ are of equal size. The three-dimensional counterpart of a _____ is a parallelepiped.
   a. 2-bridge knot
   b. Parallelogram
   c. -equivalence
   d. -module

47. The real component of a quaternion is also called its _____ part.

The term is also sometimes used informally to mean a vector, matrix, tensor, or other usually 'compound' value that is actually reduced to a single component. Thus, for example, the product of a 1×n matrix and an n×1 matrix, which is formally a 1×1 matrix, is often said to be a _____.

   a. Scalar
   b. Tensor product
   c. Self-adjoint
   d. Distributivity

48. In mathematics, a _____ is a collection of linear equations involving the same set of variables. For example,

$$3x + 2y - z = 1$$
$$2x - 2y + 4z = -2$$
$$-x + \tfrac{1}{2}y - z = 0$$

Chapter 3. Commutative Rings I

is a system of three equations in the three variables x, y, z. A solution to a linear system is an assignment of numbers to the variables such that all the equations are simultaneously satisfied.

- a. System of linear equations
- b. Simultaneous equations
- c. -equivalence
- d. -module

49. In mathematics, the _____ construction in abstract algebra constructs an abelian group from a commutative monoid in the best possible way. It takes its name from the more general construction in category theory, introduced by Alexander Grothendieck in his fundamental work of the mid-1950s that resulted in the development of K-theory. The _____ is denoted by K or K_0.

- a. Power set
- b. Restriction of scalars
- c. Coimage
- d. Grothendieck group

50. In linear algebra, a family of vectors is _____ if none of them can be written as a linear combination of finitely many other vectors in the collection. A family of vectors which is not _____ is called linearly dependent. For instance, in the three-dimensional real vector space $\mathbb{R}^3$ we have the following example.

- a. Composition ring
- b. Derivative algebra
- c. Grothendieck group
- d. Linearly independent

51. In mathematics, the _____ for a Euclidean space consists of one unit vector pointing in the direction of each axis of the Cartesian coordinate system. For example, the _____ for the Euclidean plane are the vectors

$$\mathbf{e}_x = (1,0), \quad \mathbf{e}_y = (0,1),$$

and the _____ for three-dimensional space are the vectors

$$\mathbf{e}_x = (1,0,0), \quad \mathbf{e}_y = (0,1,0), \quad \mathbf{e}_z = (0,0,1).$$

Here the vector e_x points in the x direction, the vector e_y points in the y direction, and the vector e_z points in the z direction. There are several common notations for these vectors, including {e_x, e_y, e_z}, {e_1, e_2, e_3}, {i, j, k}, and {x, y, z}.

- a. -module
- b. 2-bridge knot
- c. -equivalence
- d. Standard basis

52. In mathematics, the _____ of a vector space V is the cardinality (i.e. the number of vectors) of a basis of V. It is sometimes called Hamel _____ or algebraic _____ to distinguish it from other types of _____. All bases of a vector space have equal cardinality and so the _____ of a vector space is uniquely defined. The _____ of the vector space V over the field F can be written as $\dim_F(V)$ or as [V : F], read '_____ of V over F'.

- a. Partial trace
- b. Dual basis
- c. Cofactor
- d. Dimension

53. If $A_1, A_2, \ldots, A_n$ are _____ square matrices over a field, then

$$(A_1 A_2 \cdots A_n)^{-1} = A_n^{-1} A_{n-1}^{-1} \cdots A_1^{-1}.$$

It becomes evident why this is the case if one attempts to find an inverse for the product of the A_is from first principles, that is, that we wish to determine B such that

$$(A_1 A_2 \cdots A_n) B = I$$

where B is the inverse matrix of the product. To remove A_1 from the product, we can then write

$$A_1^{-1}(A_1 A_2 \cdots A_n) B = A_1^{-1} I$$

which would reduce the equation to

$$(A_2 A_3 \cdots A_n) B = A_1^{-1} I.$$

Likewise, then, from

$$A_2^{-1}(A_2 A_3 \cdots A_n) B = A_2^{-1} A_1^{-1} I$$

which simplifies to

$$(A_3 A_4 \cdots A_n) B = A_2^{-1} A_1^{-1} I.$$

If one repeat the process up to A_n, the equation becomes

$$B = A_n^{-1} A_{n-1}^{-1} \cdots A_2^{-1} A_1^{-1} I$$

$$B = A_n^{-1} A_{n-1}^{-1} \cdots A_2^{-1} A_1^{-1}$$

but B is the inverse matrix, i.e. $B = (A_1 A_2 \cdots A_n)^{-1}$ so the property is established.

Over the field of real numbers, the set of singular n-by-n matrices, considered as a subset of $R^{n \times n}$, is a null set, i.e., has Lebesgue measure zero.

a. 2-bridge knot
c. -equivalence
b. -module
d. Nonsingular

54. In linear algebra, two n-by-n matrices A and B are called _____ if

$$B = P^{-1}AP$$

for some invertible n-by-n matrix P. _____ matrices represent the same linear transformation under two different bases, with P being the change of basis matrix.

The matrix P is sometimes called a similarity transformation. In the context of matrix groups, similarity is sometimes referred to as conjugacy, with _____ matrices being conjugate.

- a. Skew-symmetric
- b. Cartan matrix
- c. Zero matrix
- d. Similar

55. In mathematics, any vector space, V, has a corresponding dual vector space (or just dual space for short) consisting of all linear functionals on V. Dual vector spaces defined on finite-dimensional vector spaces can be used for defining tensors which are studied in tensor algebra. When applied to vector spaces of functions (which typically are infinite-dimensional), _____ are employed for defining and studying concepts like measures, distributions, and Hilbert spaces. Consequently, the dual space is an important concept in the study of functional analysis.

- a. Dual spaces
- b. Conjugate transpose
- c. Barycentric coordinates
- d. Jordan normal form

56. In mathematics, a _____ is a rectangular array of numbers. This way, matrices can record data that depend on multiple parameters. In particular they are used to keep track of the coefficients of multiple linear equations. Matrices are closely connected to linear transformations, which are higher-dimensional analogs of linear functions, i.e., functions of the form f(x) = c Â· x, where c is a constant. This map corresponds to a _____ with one row and column, with entry c. In addition to a number of elementary, entrywise operations such as _____ addition a key notion is _____ multiplication, which displays a number of features not encountered in numbers; for example, products of matrices depend on the order of the factors, unlike products of real numbers, say, where c Â· d = d Â· c for any two numbers c and d.

- a. Polynomial expression
- b. Commutativity
- c. Heap
- d. Matrix

57. In linear algebra, the _____ of a matrix is the set of all possible linear combinations of its column vectors. The _____ of an m × n matrix is a subspace of m-dimensional Euclidean space. The dimension of the _____ is called the rank of the matrix.

- a. Linear inequality
- b. Pseudovector
- c. Column space
- d. Delta operator

58. In mathematics, the linear algebra concept of _____ can be applied in the context of a finite extension L/K, by using the field trace. This requires the property that the field trace $Tr_{L/K}$ provides a non-degenerate quadratic form over K. This can be guaranteed if the extension is separable; it is automatically true if K is a perfect field, and hence in the cases where K is finite, or of characteristic zero.

A _____ isn't a concrete basis like the polynomial basis or the normal basis; rather it provides a way of using a second basis for computations.

Chapter 3. Commutative Rings I

a. Linear complementarity problem
c. Column space
b. Segre classification
d. Dual basis

59. In mathematics a _____ is a construction in ring theory, quite similar to the factor groups of group theory and the quotient spaces of linear algebra. One starts with a ring R and a two-sided ideal I in R, and constructs a new ring, the _____ R/I, essentially by requiring that all elements of I be zero. Intuitively, the _____ R/I is a 'simplified version' of R where the elements of I are 'ignored'.
  a. Monoid ring
  c. Subring
  b. Domain
  d. Quotient ring

60. In abstract algebra, an _____ is a bijective map f such that both f and its inverse f^{-1} are homomorphisms, i.e., structure-preserving mappings. In the more general setting of category theory, an _____ is a morphism f:X→Y in a category for which there exists an 'inverse' f^{-1}:Y→X, with the property that both $f^{-1}f=id_X$ and $ff^{-1}=id_Y$.

Informally, an _____ is a kind of mapping between objects, which shows a relationship between two properties or operations.

  a. ADE classification
  c. Endomorphism
  b. Epimorphism
  d. Isomorphism

61. In mathematics, specifically abstract algebra, the _____ are three theorems that describe the relationship between quotients, homomorphisms, and subobjects. Versions of the theorems exist for groups, rings, vector spaces, modules, Lie algebras, and various other algebraic structures. In universal algebra, the _____ can be generalized to the context of algebras and congruences.
  a. AKS primality test
  c. ADE classification
  b. Identity theorem for Riemann surfaces
  d. Isomorphism theorems

62. Model theory generalizes the notion of _____ to arbitrary theories: an embedding of M into N is called an _____ if for every x in N there is a formula p with parameters in M, such that p(x) is true and the set

  {y in N | p(y)}

is finite. It turns out that applying this definition to the theory of fields gives the usual definition of _____. The Galois group of N over M can again be defined as the group of automorphisms, and it turns out that most of the theory of Galois groups can be developed for the general case.

  a. Iwasawa theory
  c. Equivariant L-function
  b. Algebraic closure
  d. Algebraic extension

63. The _____ and descending chain condition (DCC) are finiteness properties satisfied by certain algebraic structures, most importantly, ideals in a commutative ring. These conditions played an important role in the development of the structure theory of commutative rings in the works of David Hilbert, Emmy Noether, and Emil Artin. The conditions themselves can be stated in an abstract form, so that they make sense for any partially ordered set.
  a. Invariant polynomial
  c. Atomic domain
  b. Integral
  d. Ascending chain condition

Chapter 3. Commutative Rings I

64. In algebraic topology, a simplicial k-_____ is a formal linear combination of k-simplices.

Integration is defined on chains by taking the linear combination of integrals over the simplices in the _____ with coefficients typically integers. The set of all k-chains forms a group and the sequence of these groups is called a _____ complex.

- a. Tesseract
- b. Combinatorial topology
- c. Bockstein homomorphism
- d. Chain

65. In mathematics, if L is a field extension of K, then an element a of L is called an _____ over K if there exists some non-zero polynomial g(x) with coefficients in K such that g(a)=0. Elements of L which are not algebraic over K are called transcendental over K.

These notions generalize the algebraic numbers and the transcendental numbers (where the field extension is C/Q, C being the field of complex numbers and Q being the field of rational numbers.)

- a. Affine Hecke algebra
- b. Algebraic element
- c. Indeterminate
- d. Inverse element

66. In field theory, given a field extension E / F and an element α of E which is an algebraic element over F, the _____ of α is the monic polynomial p, with coefficients in F, of least degree such that p(α) = 0. The _____ is irreducible over F, and any other non-zero polynomial f with f(α) = 0 is a (polynomial) multiple of p.

For example, for $F = \mathbb{Q}, E = \mathbb{R}, \alpha = \sqrt{2}$ the _____ for α is p(x) = x^2 - 2.

- a. Vandermonde polynomial
- b. Kazhdan-Lusztig polynomials
- c. Ring of symmetric functions
- d. Minimal polynomial

67. In mathematics, a field F is said to be _____ if every polynomial in one variable of degree at least 1, with coefficients in F, has a root in F.

As an example, the field of real numbers is not _____, because the polynomial equation x^2 + 1 = 0 has no solution in real numbers, even though all its coefficients (1 and 0) are real. The same argument proves that no subfield of the real field is _____; in particular, the field of rational numbers is not _____.

- a. Inverse semigroup
- b. Unique factorization domain
- c. Ordered exponential
- d. Algebraically closed

Chapter 4. Fields

1. The set of all symmetry operations considered, on all objects in a set X, can be modeled as a group action g : G × X → X, where the image of g in G and x in X is written as gÂ·x. If, for some g, gÂ·x = y then x and y are said to be symmetrical to each other. For each object x, operations g for which gÂ·x = x form a group, the _____ of the object, a subgroup of G. If the _____ of x is the trivial group then x is said to be asymmetric, otherwise symmetric.

   a. 2-bridge knot
   b. -module
   c. -equivalence
   d. Symmetry group

2. A _____ of n variables is one whose value at any n-tuple of arguments is the same as its value at any permutation of that n-tuple. While this notion can apply to any type of function whose n arguments live in the same set, it is most often used for polynomial functions, in which case these are the functions given by symmetric polynomials. There is very little systematic theory of symmetric non-polynomial functions of n variables, so this sense is little-used, except as a general definition.

   a. Symmetric function
   b. Symmetrization
   c. -module
   d. -equivalence

3. In mathematics, an _____ is an isomorphism from a mathematical object to itself. It is, in some sense, a symmetry of the object, and a way of mapping the object to itself while preserving all of its structure. The set of all automorphisms of an object forms a group, called the _____ group.

   a. Endomorphism
   b. Epimorphism
   c. ADE classification
   d. Automorphism

4. In abstract algebra, a _____ is an algebraic structure with notions of addition, subtraction, multiplication and division, satisfying certain axioms. The most commonly used fields are the _____ of real numbers, the _____ of complex numbers, and the _____ of rational numbers, but there are also finite fields, fields of functions, various algebraic number fields, p-adic fields, and so forth.

   Any _____ may be used as the scalars for a vector space, which is the standard general context for linear algebra.

   a. Generic polynomial
   b. Field
   c. Tensor product of fields
   d. Separable

5. In mathematics, a _____ is a group associated with a certain type of field extension. The study of field extensions (and polynomials which give rise to them) via Galois groups is called Galois theory after Évariste Galois who first invented them

   a. Splitting field
   b. Primitive element theorem
   c. Field of fractions
   d. Galois group

6. A _____ is a set G closed under a binary operation · satisfying the following 3 axioms:

   - Associativity: For all a, b and c in G, (a · b) · c = a · (b · c.)
   - Identity element: There exists an e∈G such that for all a in G, e · a = a · e = a.
   - Inverse element: For each a in G, there is an element b in G such that a · b = b · a = e, where e is an identity element.

Basic examples for groups are the integers Z with addition operation, or rational numbers without zero Q{0} with multiplication. More generally, for any ring R, the units in R form a multiplicative _____ Groups include, however, much more general structures than the above.

Chapter 4. Fields

   a. Nilpotent group
   b. Grigorchuk group
   c. Product of group subsets
   d. Group

7. In mathematics, the _____ of a ring R, often denoted char(R), is defined to be the smallest number of times one must add the ring's multiplicative identity element (1) to itself to get the additive identity element (0); the ring is said to have _____ zero if this repeated sum never reaches the additive identity. That is, char(R) is the smallest positive number n such that

$$\underbrace{1 + \cdots + 1}_{n \text{ summands}} = 0$$

if such a number n exists, and 0 otherwise. The _____ may also be taken to be the exponent of the ring's additive group, that is, the smallest positive n such that

$$\underbrace{a + \cdots + a}_{n \text{ summands}} = 0$$

for every element a of the ring (again, if n exists; otherwise zero.)

   a. Free ideal ring
   b. Coherent ring
   c. Hereditary
   d. Characteristic

8. In mathematics, a polynomial P(X) is _____ over a field K if all of its irreducible factors have distinct roots in an algebraic closure of K - that is each irreducible factor of P(X) has distinct linear factors in some large enough field extension. There is, however, another, non-equivalent definition of separability. It says that P is _____ if and only if it is coprime to its formal derivative P'.
   a. Transcendence degree
   b. Global field
   c. Field of fractions
   d. Separable

9. In mathematics, the adjective _____ means that an object cannot be expressed as a product of more than one non-trivial factors in a given set. See also factorization.

For any field F, the ring of polynomials with coefficients in F is denoted by F[x].

   a. Ehrhart polynomial
   b. Irreducible
   c. Integer-valued polynomial
   d. Alternating polynomial

10. The _____ of a Lie algebra $\mathfrak{g}$ is a particular ideal of $\mathfrak{g}$.

Let $\mathfrak{g}$ be a Lie algebra. The _____ of $\mathfrak{g}$ is defined as the largest solvable ideal of $\mathfrak{g}$.

   a. Radical
   b. Class sum
   c. Cyclically reduced word
   d. Garside element

Chapter 4. Fields

11. In algebra, _____ is one of the cases that may arise in attempting to solve a cubic equation with integer coefficients with roots that are expressed with radicals. Specifically, if a cubic polynomial is irreducible over the rational numbers and has three real roots, then in order to express the roots with radicals, one must introduce complex-valued expressions, even though the resulting expressions are ultimately real-valued. _____ was the original reason for the introduction of the complex number system by Niccolò Fontana Tartaglia and Gerolamo Cardano in 1545.

   a. Reduced ring
   b. Birational invariant
   c. Casus irreducibilis
   d. Tight closure

12. _____ or biquadratic reciprocity is a collection of theorems in elementary and algebraic number theory that state conditions under which the congruence $x^4 \equiv p \pmod{q}$ is solvable; the word 'reciprocity' comes from the form of some of these theorems, in that they relate the solvability of the congruence $x^4 \equiv p \pmod{q}$ to that of $x^4 \equiv q \pmod{p}$.

Euler made the first conjectures about biquadratic reciprocity. Gauss published two monographs on biquadratic reciprocity.

   a. Cyclotomic character
   b. Modulus
   c. Herbrand quotient
   d. Quartic

13. In abstract algebra, an algebraic field extension L/K is said to be normal if L is the splitting field of a family of polynomials in K[X]. Bourbaki calls such an extension a quasi-Galois extension.

The normality of L/K is equivalent to each of the following properties:

- Let K^a be an algebraic closure of K containing L. Every embedding σ of L in K^a which restricts to the identity on K, satisfies σ(L) = L. In other words, σ is an automorphism of L over K.
- Every irreducible polynomial in K[X] which has a root in L factors into linear factors in L[X].

For example, $\mathbb{Q}(\sqrt{2})$ is a _____ of $\mathbb{Q}$, since it is the splitting field of $x^2 - 2$. On the other hand, $\mathbb{Q}(\sqrt[3]{2})$ is not a _____ of $\mathbb{Q}$ since the polynomial $x^3 - 2$ has one root in it (namely, $\sqrt[3]{2}$), but not all of them (it does not have the non-real cubic roots of 2.)

   a. Normal extension
   b. Dimension theorem for vector spaces
   c. Semifield
   d. Matrix

14. In mathematics, a _____ is an algebraic structure whose main use is in studying geometric objects such as Lie groups and differentiable manifolds. Lie algebras were introduced to study the concept of infinitesimal transformations. The term '_____') was introduced by Hermann Weyl in the 1930s.

   a. Maximal torus
   b. Lorentz group
   c. Lie algebra
   d. Weyl group

15. In mathematics, a _____ is (most commonly) a special kind of function from a group to a field (such as the complex numbers.) There are at least two distinct, but overlapping meanings. Other uses of the word '_____' are almost always qualified.

a. Real representation
b. Deligne-Lusztig theory
c. Trivial representation
d. Character

16. In mathematics, more specifically in abstract algebra, _____ provides a connection between field theory and group theory. Using _____, certain problems in field theory can be reduced to group theory, which is in some sense simpler and better understood.

Originally Galois used permutation groups to describe how the various roots of a given polynomial equation are related to each other.

a. Galois group
b. Separable
c. Simple extension
d. Galois theory

17. In mathematics, especially in the area of abstract algebra known as ring theory, a _____ is a ring with 0 ≠ 1 such that ab = 0 implies that either a = 0 or b = 0 (the zero-product property.) That is, it is a nontrivial ring without left or right zero divisors. A commutative _____ is called an integral _____.

a. Subring
b. Coherent ring
c. Partially-ordered ring
d. Domain

18. In mathematics, _____ or factoring is the decomposition of an object ' href='/wiki/Matrix_(mathematics)'>matrix) into a product of other objects, or factors, which when multiplied together give the original. For example, the number 15 factors into primes as 3 × 5, and the polynomial $x^2 - 4$ factors as (x − 2)(x + 2.) In all cases, a product of simpler objects is obtained.

a. 2-bridge knot
b. Factorization
c. -equivalence
d. -module

19. In mathematics, a _____ is, roughly speaking, a commutative ring in which every element, with special exceptions, can be uniquely written as a product of prime elements, analogous to the fundamental theorem of arithmetic for the integers. Unique factorization domains are sometimes called factorial rings, following the terminology of Bourbaki.

Note that unique factorization domains appear in the following chain of class inclusions:

- Commutative rings >⊃ integral domains >⊃ unique factorization domains >⊃ principal ideal domains >⊃ Euclidean domains >⊃ fields

a. Unit ring
b. Isomorphism class
c. Unique factorization domain
d. Absorption law

20. In mathematics, a _____ is a partially ordered set in which subsets of any two elements have a unique supremum and an infimum Lattices can also be characterized as algebraic structures satisfying certain axiomatic identities. Since the two definitions are equivalent, _____ theory draws on both order theory and universal algebra.

a. -equivalence
b. Lattice of subgroups
c. Lattice
d. -module

Chapter 4. Fields

21. In abstract algebra, the concept of a _____ over a ring is a generalization of the notion of vector space, where instead of requiring the scalars to lie in a field, the 'scalars' may lie in an arbitrary ring. Modules also generalize the notion of abelian groups, which are modules over $\mathbb{Z}$.

Thus, a _____, like a vector space, is an additive abelian group; a product is defined between elements of the ring and elements of the _____, and this multiplication is associative (when used with the multiplication in the ring) and distributive.

a. Near-field
b. Semigroupoid
c. Module
d. Goodman-Nguyen-van Fraassen algebra

22. In mathematics, the term _____ is used to describe an algebraic structures which in some sense cannot be divided by a smaller structure of the same type. Put another way, an algebraic structure is _____ if the kernel of every homomorphism is either the whole structure or a single element. Some examples are:

- A group is called a _____ group if it does not contain a non-trivial proper normal subgroup.
- A ring is called a _____ ring if it does not contain a non-trivial two sided ideal.
- A module is called a _____ module if does not contain a non-trivial submodule.
- An algebra is called a _____ algebra if does not contain a non-trivial two sided ideal.

The general pattern is that the structure admits no non-trivial congruence relations.

a. Linear combinations
b. Simple
c. Polarization identity
d. Commutativity

23. In mathematics, more specifically in field theory, a _____ is a field extension which is generated by the adjunction of a single element. Simple extensions are well understood and can be completely classified.

The primitive element theorem provides a characterization of the finite extensions which are simple.

a. Tensor product of fields
b. Degree of a field extension
c. P-adic number
d. Simple extension

24. In linear algebra, functional analysis and related areas of mathematics, a _____ is a function that assigns a strictly positive length or size to all vectors in a vector space, other than the zero vector. A seminorm (or pseudonorm), on the other hand, is allowed to assign zero length to some non-zero vectors.

A simple example is the 2-dimensional Euclidean space R^2 equipped with the Euclidean _____.

a. Norm
b. Quasinorm
c. -module
d. -equivalence

25. In algebra, the _____ of a polynomial with real or complex coefficients is a certain expression in the coefficients of the polynomial which is a symmetric polynomial in the coefficients and gives information on the nature of the roots; in particular, it is equal to zero if and only if the polynomial has a multiple root (i.e. a root with multiplicity greater than one) in the complex numbers. For example, the _____ of the quadratic polynomial

$ax^2 + bx + c$ is $b^2 - 4ac$.

The _____ of the cubic polynomial

$$ax^3 + bx^2 + cx + d \text{ is } b^2c^2 - 4ac^3 - 4b^3d - 27a^2d^2 + 18abcd$$

a. Discriminant
b. Minimal polynomial
c. Polynomial remainder theorem
d. Kazhdan-Lusztig polynomials

26. In mathematics, the _____ concerns whether or not every finite group appears as the Galois group of some Galois extension of the rational numbers Q. This problem, first posed in the 19th century, is unsolved.

More generally, let G be a given finite group, and let K be a field. Then the question is this: is there a Galois extension field L/K such that the Galois group of the extension is isomorphic to G? One says that G is realizable over K if such a field L exists.

a. ADE classification
b. Inverse Galois problem
c. Abelian P-root group
d. AKS primality test

27. In linear algebra, the _____ of an n-by-n square matrix A is defined to be the sum of the elements on the main diagonal (the diagonal from the upper left to the lower right) of A, i.e.,

$$\text{tr}(A) = a_{11} + a_{22} + \cdots + a_{nn} = \sum_{i=1}^{n} a_{ii}$$

where a_{ij} represents the entry on the ith row and jth column of A. Equivalently, the _____ of a matrix is the sum of its eigenvalues, making it an invariant with respect to a change of basis. This characterization can be used to define the _____ for a linear operator in general.

Note that the _____ is only defined for a square matrix (i.e. n×n.)

a. Coefficient matrix
b. Trace
c. Defective matrix
d. Dot product

Chapter 5. Groups II

1. An _____ is a group satisfying the requirement that the result of applying the group operation to two group elements does not depend on their order Abelian groups generalize the arithmetic of addition of integers; they are named after Niels Henrik Abel.

The concept of an _____ is one of the first concepts encountered in undergraduate abstract algebra, with many other basic objects, such as a module and a vector space, being its refinements.

   a. Abelian group
   b. ADE classification
   c. Elementary abelian group
   d. Algebraically compact

2. In abstract algebra, the _____ is a construction which combines several modules into a new, larger module. The result of the direct summation of modules is the 'smallest general' module which contains the given modules as subspaces. This is an example of a coproduct.
   a. Schmidt decomposition
   b. Frame
   c. Finite dimensional von Neumann algebra
   d. Direct sum

3. A _____ is a set G closed under a binary operation · satisfying the following 3 axioms:

   - Associativity: For all a, b and c in G, (a · b) · c = a · (b · c).
   - Identity element: There exists an e∈G such that for all a in G, e · a = a · e = a.
   - Inverse element: For each a in G, there is an element b in G such that a · b = b · a = e, where e is an identity element.

Basic examples for groups are the integers Z with addition operation, or rational numbers without zero Q{0} with multiplication. More generally, for any ring R, the units in R form a multiplicative _____ Groups include, however, much more general structures than the above.

   a. Grigorchuk group
   b. Group
   c. Product of group subsets
   d. Nilpotent group

4. In linear algebra and functional analysis, a _____ is a linear transformation P from a vector space to itself such that $P^2 = P$. It leaves its image unchanged. Though abstract, this definition of '_____' formalizes and generalizes the idea of graphical _____.
   a. Convolution power
   b. Projection
   c. C_0-semigroup
   d. Lumer-Phillips theorem

5. In mathematics, in the field of group theory, a _____ of a finite group is a quasisimple subnormal subgroup. Any two distinct components commute. The product of all the components is the layer of the group.
   a. Stallings' theorem about ends of groups
   b. Group homomorphism
   c. Component
   d. Wreath product

6. In linear algebra, a _____ is a set of vectors that, in a linear combination, can represent every vector in a given vector space or free module, and such that no element of the set can be represented as a linear combination of the others. In other words, a _____ is a linearly independent spanning set.
   a. Minor
   b. Chirality
   c. Supergroup
   d. Basis

7. In mathematics, especially in the area of algebra studying the theory of abelian groups, a _____ is a generalization of direct summand. It has found many uses in abelian group theory and related areas.

A subgroup S of a (typically abelian) group G is said to be pure if whenever an element of S has an nth root in G, it necessarily has an nth root in S.

- a. -module
- b. -equivalence
- c. 2-bridge knot
- d. Pure subgroup

8. In mathematics, especially in the area of abstract algebra known as ring theory, a _____ is a ring with $0 \neq 1$ such that $ab = 0$ implies that either $a = 0$ or $b = 0$ (the zero-product property.) That is, it is a nontrivial ring without left or right zero divisors. A commutative _____ is called an integral _____.

- a. Domain
- b. Subring
- c. Coherent ring
- d. Partially-ordered ring

9. In mathematics, _____ or factoring is the decomposition of an object ' href='/wiki/Matrix_(mathematics)'>matrix) into a product of other objects, or factors, which when multiplied together give the original. For example, the number 15 factors into primes as 3 × 5, and the polynomial $x^2 - 4$ factors as $(x - 2)(x + 2)$. In all cases, a product of simpler objects is obtained.

- a. -equivalence
- b. Factorization
- c. 2-bridge knot
- d. -module

10. In mathematics, a _____ is, roughly speaking, a commutative ring in which every element, with special exceptions, can be uniquely written as a product of prime elements, analogous to the fundamental theorem of arithmetic for the integers. Unique factorization domains are sometimes called factorial rings, following the terminology of Bourbaki.

Note that unique factorization domains appear in the following chain of class inclusions:

- Commutative rings >⊃ integral domains >⊃ unique factorization domains >⊃ principal ideal domains >⊃ Euclidean domains >⊃ fields

- a. Unique factorization domain
- b. Absorption law
- c. Unit ring
- d. Isomorphism class

11. In algebraic geometry, divisors are a generalization of codimension one subvarieties of algebraic varieties; two different generalizations are in common use, Cartier divisors and Weil divisors The concepts agree on non-singular varieties over algebraically closed fields.

A Weil _____ is a locally finite linear combination (with integral coefficients) of irreducible subvarieties of codimension one.

- a. Picard group
- b. Divisor
- c. Linear system of divisors
- d. Lefschetz pencil

12. In algebra, the _____ of a module over a principal ideal domain occur in one form of the structure theorem for finitely generated modules over a principal ideal domain.

If R is a PID and M a finitely generated R-module, then M is isomorphic to a unique sum of the form

$$M \cong R^r \oplus \bigoplus_i R/(q_i)$$

where $q_i \neq 1$ and the (q_i) are primary ideals.

The ideals (q_i) are unique (up to order); the elements q_i are unique up to associatedness, and are called the _____.

a. Elementary divisors
c. Extension of scalars
b. Injective hull
d. Invariant factors

13. In mathematics, the _____ of a ring R, often denoted char(R), is defined to be the smallest number of times one must add the ring's multiplicative identity element (1) to itself to get the additive identity element (0); the ring is said to have _____ zero if this repeated sum never reaches the additive identity. That is, char(R) is the smallest positive number n such that

$$\underbrace{1 + \cdots + 1}_{n \text{ summands}} = 0$$

if such a number n exists, and 0 otherwise. The _____ may also be taken to be the exponent of the ring's additive group, that is, the smallest positive n such that

$$\underbrace{a + \cdots + a}_{n \text{ summands}} = 0$$

for every element a of the ring (again, if n exists; otherwise zero.)

a. Free ideal ring
c. Coherent ring
b. Characteristic
d. Hereditary

14. The _____ of a module over a principal ideal domain occur in one form of the structure theorem for finitely generated modules over a principal ideal domain.

If R is a PID and M a finitely generated R-module, then

$$M \cong R^r \oplus R/(a_1) \oplus R/(a_2) \oplus \cdots \oplus R/(a_m)$$

for some $r \in \mathbb{Z}_0^+$ and nonzero elements $a_1, \ldots, a_m \in R$ for which $a_1 \mid \cdots \mid a_m$. The nonnegative integer r is called the free rank or Betti number of the module M, while $a_1, \ldots, a_m$ are the _____ of M and are unique up to associatedness.

- a. Extension of scalars
- b. Injective hull
- c. Invariant basis number
- d. Invariant factors

15. In abstract algebra, the term _____ refers to a number of concepts related to elements of finite order in groups and to the failure of modules to be free.

Let G be a group. An element g of G is called a _____ element if g has finite order.

- a. Torsion subgroup
- b. Divisible group
- c. Cyclic group
- d. Torsion

16. In the theory of abelian groups, the _____ A_T of an abelian group A is the subgroup of A consisting of all elements that have finite order. An abelian group A is called a torsion (or periodic) group if every element of A has finite order and is called torsion-free if every element of A except the identity is of infinite order.

The proof that A_T is closed under addition relies on the commutativity of addition

- a. Locally cyclic group
- b. Divisible group
- c. Cyclic group
- d. Torsion subgroup

17. In abstract algebra, the concept of a _____ over a ring is a generalization of the notion of vector space, where instead of requiring the scalars to lie in a field, the 'scalars' may lie in an arbitrary ring. Modules also generalize the notion of abelian groups, which are modules over $\mathbb{Z}$.

Thus, a _____, like a vector space, is an additive abelian group; a product is defined between elements of the ring and elements of the _____, and this multiplication is associative (when used with the multiplication in the ring) and distributive.

- a. Goodman-Nguyen-van Fraassen algebra
- b. Near-field
- c. Semigroupoid
- d. Module

18. The iterated wreath products of cyclic groups of order p are very important examples of _____. Denote the cyclic group of order p as W(1), and the wreath product of W(n) with W(1) as W(n+1.) Then W(n) is the Sylow p-subgroup of the symmetric group Sym(p^n.)
- a. Group representations
- b. Polycyclic group
- c. History of group theory
- d. P-groups

19. In mathematics, a _____ is an algebraic structure whose main use is in studying geometric objects such as Lie groups and differentiable manifolds. Lie algebras were introduced to study the concept of infinitesimal transformations. The term '_____') was introduced by Hermann Weyl in the 1930s.

Chapter 5. Groups II

a. Lorentz group
b. Weyl group
c. Maximal torus
d. Lie algebra

20. In mathematics, particularly in the area of abstract algebra known as group theory, a _____ is a subgroup that is invariant under all automorphisms of the parent group. Because conjugation is an automorphism, every _____ is normal, though not every normal subgroup is characteristic. Examples of characteristic subgroups include the commutator subgroup and the center of a group.

a. Principal homogeneous space
b. Group object
c. Composition series
d. Characteristic subgroup

21. In abstract algebra, a _____ provides a way to break up an algebraic structure, such as a group or a module, into simple pieces. The need for considering _____ in the context of modules arises from the fact that many naturally occurring modules are not semisimple, hence cannot be decomposed into a direct sum of simple modules. A _____ of a module M is a finite increasing filtration of M by submodules such that the successive quotients are simple and serves as a replacement of the direct sum decomposition of M into its simple constituents.

a. Baby-step giant-step
b. Conjugacy class
c. Composition series
d. Burnside's theorem

22. In mathematics, the _____ gives an indication of the extent to which a certain binary operation fails to be commutative. There are different definitions used in group theory and ring theory.

The _____ of two elements, g and h, of a group, G, is the element

$[g, h] = g^{-1}h^{-1}gh$

It is equal to the group's identity if and only if g and h commute (i.e., if and only if gh = hg.)

a. Commutator
b. Coimage
c. Linear combinations
d. Dimension theorem for vector spaces

23. In mathematics, there are several meanings of _____ depending on the subject.

A _____, usually denoted by ° (the _____ symbol), is a measurement of plane angle, representing $1/360$ of a full rotation. When that angle is with respect to a reference meridian, it indicates a location along a great circle of a sphere, such as Earth, Mars, or the celestial sphere.

a. Median algebra
b. Degree
c. Relation algebra
d. Symmetric difference

24. A _____ is a symbol that stands for a value that may vary; the term usually occurs in opposition to constant, which is a symbol for a non-varying value, i.e. completely fixed or fixed in the context of use. The concepts of constants and variables are fundamental to all modern mathematics, science, engineering, and computer programming.

Much of the basic theory for which we use variables today, such as school geometry and algebra, was developed thousands of years ago, but the use of symbolic formulae and variables is only several hundreds of years old.

a. Variable
b. -equivalence
c. 2-bridge knot
d. -module

25. In mathematics, especially in the fields of group theory and Lie theory, a _____ is a kind of normal series of subgroups or Lie subalgebras, expressing the idea that the commutator is nearly trivial. For groups, this is an explicit expression that the group is a nilpotent group, and for matrix rings, this is an explicit expression that in some basis the matrix ring consists entirely of upper triangular matrices with constant diagonal

a. Fitting length
b. Central series
c. Rank of a group
d. Quaternion group

26. In mathematics, an element x of a ring R is called _____ if there exists some positive integer n such that $x^n = 0$.

The term was introduced by Benjamin Peirce in the context of elements of an algebra that vanish when raised to a power.

- This definition can be applied in particular to square matrices. The matrix

$$A = \begin{pmatrix} 0 & 1 & 0 \\ 0 & 0 & 1 \\ 0 & 0 & 0 \end{pmatrix}$$

is _____ because $A^3 = 0$. See _____ matrix for more.

a. Nilpotent
b. Ring of integers
c. Product ring
d. Hochschild homology

27. In mathematics, the _____ Φ(G) of a group G is the intersection of G and all proper maximal subgroups of G. So if G has no proper maximal subgroups, then Φ(G) is G itself. It is analogous to the Jacobson radical in the theory of commutative rings, and intuitively can be thought of as the subgroup of 'small elements' It is named after Giovanni Frattini, who defined the concept in a paper published in 1885.

a. Double coset
b. Fitting length
c. Group action
d. Frattini subgroup

28. In mathematics the _____ is a property that a binary operation can satisfy which determines how the order of evaluation behaves for the given operation. Unlike for associative operations, order of evaluation is significant for operations satisfying _____.

A binary operation * on a set S possessing a commutative binary operation + , satisfies the _____ if

$$a * (b * c) + c * (a * b) + b * (c * a) = 0 \quad \forall a, b, c \in S.$$

In a Lie algebra, the objects that obey the _____ are infinitesimal motions.

a. Nilpotent orbit
b. Knizhnik-Zamolodchikov equations
c. Lie ring
d. Jacobi identity

29. The group (Z,+) of integers is free; we can take S = {1}. A _____ on a two-element set S occurs in the proof of the Banach-Tarski paradox and is described there.

On the other hand, any nontrivial finite group cannot be free, since the elements of a free generating set of a _____ have infinite order.

a. Baby-step giant-step
b. Class function
c. Fitting length
d. Free group

30. _____, in mathematics, are a non-commutative number system that extends the complex numbers. The _____ were first described by Irish mathematician Sir William Rowan Hamilton in 1843 and applied to mechanics in three-dimensional space. They find uses in both theoretical and applied mathematics, in particular for calculations involving three-dimensional rotations , such as in 3D computer graphics, although they have been superseded in many applications by vectors and matrices.

a. Generalized quaternion interpolation
b. Split-quaternions
c. Split-biquaternion
d. Quaternions

31. In mathematics, the _____ construction in abstract algebra constructs an abelian group from a commutative monoid in the best possible way. It takes its name from the more general construction in category theory, introduced by Alexander Grothendieck in his fundamental work of the mid-1950s that resulted in the development of K-theory. The _____ is denoted by K or K_0.

a. Coimage
b. Restriction of scalars
c. Grothendieck group
d. Power set

32. In abstract algebra, the _____ of a module is a measure of the module's 'size'. It is defined as the _____ of the longest ascending chain of submodules and is a generalization of the concept of dimension for vector spaces. The modules with finite _____ share many important properties with finite-dimensional vector spaces.

a. Length
b. Supermodule
c. Finitely generated module
d. Morita equivalence

33. A _____ between two algebras over a field K, A and B, is a map $F : A \to B$ such that for all k in K and x,y in A,

- F(kx) = kF(x)

- F(x + y) = F(x) + F(y)

- F(xy) = F(x)F(y)

If F is bijective then F is said to be an isomorphism between A and B.

Let A = K[x] be the set of all polynomials over a field K and B be the set of all polynomial functions over K. Both A and B are algebras over K given by the standard multiplication and addition of polynomials and functions, respectively. We can map each f in A to $\hat{f}$ in B by the rule $\hat{f}(t) = f(t)$. A routine check shows that the mapping $f \mapsto \hat{f}$ is a _____ of the algebras A and B. If K is a finite field then let

$$p(x) = \Pi_{t \in K}(x - t).$$

p is a nonzero polynomial in K[x], however $p(t) = 0$ for all t in K, so $\hat{p} = 0$ is the zero function and the algebras are not isomorphic.

- a. Tensor algebra
- b. Homomorphism
- c. Tensor product of algebras
- d. Frobenius matrix

34. In abstract algebra, a branch of mathematics, a _____ is an algebraic structure with a single, associative binary operation and an identity element. Monoids occur in a number of branches of mathematics and capture the idea of function composition; indeed, this notion is abstracted in category theory, where the _____ is a category with one object. Monoids are also commonly used to provide an algebraic foundation for computer science; in this case, the transition _____ and syntactic _____ are used in describing a finite state machine, whereas trace monoids and history monoids provide a foundation for process calculi and concurrent computing.
- a. Rupture field
- b. Goodman-Nguyen-van Fraassen algebra
- c. Precedence rule
- d. Monoid

35. In mathematics, a _____ is an algebraic structure consisting of a nonempty set S together with an associative binary operation. In other words, a _____ is an associative magma. The terminology is derived from the anterior notion of a group.
- a. Regular semigroup
- b. Semigroup
- c. Syndetic set
- d. Free monoid

36. In mathematics, one method of defining a group is by a _____. One specifies a set S of generators so that every element of the group can be written as a product of some of these generators, and a set R of relations among those generators. We then say G has _____

$$\langle S \mid R \rangle.$$

Informally, G has the above _____ if it is the 'freest group' generated by S subject only to the relations R. Formally, the group G is said to have the above _____ if it is isomorphic to the quotient of a free group on S by the normal subgroup generated by the relations R.

- a. -equivalence
- b. Tietze transformations
- c. Presentation
- d. -module

Chapter 6. Commutative Rings II

1. In mathematics, a _____ is a type of algebraic structure. There is some variation among mathematicians as to exactly what properties a _____ is required to have, as described in detail below. However, commonly a _____ is defined as a set together with two binary operations (usually called addition and multiplication), where each operation combines two elements to form a third element.
   a. Ring
   b. 2-bridge knot
   c. -module
   d. -equivalence

2. In mathematics, a _____ is an algebraic structure whose main use is in studying geometric objects such as Lie groups and differentiable manifolds. Lie algebras were introduced to study the concept of infinitesimal transformations. The term '_____') was introduced by Hermann Weyl in the 1930s.
   a. Weyl group
   b. Lie algebra
   c. Lorentz group
   d. Maximal torus

3. In ring theory, a branch of abstract algebra, an _____ is a special subset of a ring. The _____ concept generalizes in an appropriate way some important properties of integers like 'even number' or 'multiple of 3'.

For instance, in rings one studies prime ideals instead of prime numbers, one defines coprime ideals as a generalization of coprime numbers, and one can prove a generalized Chinese remainder theorem about ideals.

   a. Augmentation ideal
   b. Ideal
   c. AKS primality test
   d. ADE classification

4. In mathematics, a _____ is a subset of a ring which shares many important properties of a prime number in the ring of integers Prime ideals in order theory are treated in the article on ideals in order theory.
   a. Principal ideal
   b. Prime ideal
   c. Radical of an ring
   d. Radical of an ideal

5. In mathematics, more specifically in ring theory, a _____ is an ideal which is maximal (with respect to set inclusion) amongst all proper ideals, i.e. which is not contained in any other proper ideal of the ring.

Maximal ideals are important because the quotient rings of maximal ideals are simple rings, and in the special case of unital commutative rings they are also fields. Rings which contain only one _____ are called local rings.

   a. Jacobson radical
   b. Principal ideal
   c. Radical of an ring
   d. Maximal ideal

6. The _____ is a result about congruences in number theory and its generalizations in abstract algebra.

The original form of the theorem, contained in a third-century AD book Sun Zi suanjing by Chinese mathematician Sun Tzu and later republished in a 1247 book by Qin Jiushao, the Shushu Jiuzhang (æ•¸æ›¸ä¹ ç« Mathematical Treatise in Nine Sections) is a statement about simultaneous congruences

Suppose n_1, n_2, â€¦, n_k are positive integers which are pairwise coprime.

a. Modular arithmetic
c. Discrete logarithm
b. Multiplicative group of integers modulo n
d. Chinese remainder theorem

7. In ring theory, a branch of abstract algebra, a _____ is a ring in which the multiplication operation is commutative. The study of commutative rings is called commutative algebra.

Some specific kinds of commutative rings are given with the following chain of class inclusions:

- commutative rings ⊃ integral domains ⊃ unique factorization domains ⊃ principal ideal domains ⊃ Euclidean domains ⊃ fields

A ring is a set R equipped with two binary operations, i.e. operations that combine any two elements of the ring to a third. They are called addition and multiplication and commonly denoted by '+' and '·', e.g. a + b and a · b.

a. Going up
c. Commutative ring
b. Nilradical
d. Differential calculus over commutative algebras

8. In mathematics, especially in the area of abstract algebra known as ring theory, a _____ is a ring with 0 ≠ 1 such that ab = 0 implies that either a = 0 or b = 0 (the zero-product property.) That is, it is a nontrivial ring without left or right zero divisors. A commutative _____ is called an integral _____.

a. Subring
c. Partially-ordered ring
b. Coherent ring
d. Domain

9. In mathematics, _____ or factoring is the decomposition of an object ' href='/wiki/Matrix_(mathematics)'>matrix) into a product of other objects, or factors, which when multiplied together give the original. For example, the number 15 factors into primes as 3 × 5, and the polynomial $x^2 - 4$ factors as (x − 2)(x + 2.) In all cases, a product of simpler objects is obtained.

a. Factorization
c. 2-bridge knot
b. -module
d. -equivalence

10. In mathematics, a _____ is, roughly speaking, a commutative ring in which every element, with special exceptions, can be uniquely written as a product of prime elements, analogous to the fundamental theorem of arithmetic for the integers. Unique factorization domains are sometimes called factorial rings, following the terminology of Bourbaki.

Note that unique factorization domains appear in the following chain of class inclusions:

- Commutative rings >⊃ integral domains >⊃ unique factorization domains >⊃ principal ideal domains >⊃ Euclidean domains >⊃ fields

a. Absorption law
c. Unit ring
b. Unique factorization domain
d. Isomorphism class

11. In mathematics, a _____ R is a ring (with identity) for which $x^2 = x$ for all x in R; that is, R consists only of idempotent elements.

Chapter 6. Commutative Rings II

Boolean rings are automatically commutative and of characteristic 2 A _____ is essentially the same thing as a Boolean algebra, with ring multiplication corresponding to conjunction or meet ∧, and ring addition to exclusive disjunction or symmetric difference (not disjunction ∨.)

a. Domain
c. Hereditary
b. Ring of integers
d. Boolean ring

12. In mathematics, a _____ on a field k is a function

$$\nu : k \to \mathbb{Z} \cup \{\infty\}$$

satisfying the conditions

$$\nu(x \cdot y) = \nu(x) + \nu(y)$$
$$\nu(x + y) \geq \min\{\nu(x), \nu(y)\}$$
$$\nu(x) = \infty \iff x = 0$$

Note that often the trivial valuation which takes on only the values $0, \infty$ is explicitly excluded.

To every field with _____ v we can associate the subring

$$\mathcal{O}_k := \{x \in k \mid \nu(x) \geq 0\}$$

of k, which is a _____ ring.

a. Commutative ring
c. Discrete valuation
b. Going up
d. Nilradical

13. In abstract algebra, a _____ is a principal ideal domain (PID) with exactly one non-zero maximal ideal.

This means a _____ is an integral domain R which satisfies any one of the following equivalent conditions:

1. R is a local principal ideal domain, and not a field.
2. R is a valuation ring with a value group isomorphic to the integers under addition.
3. R is a local Dedekind domain and not a field.
4. R is a noetherian local ring with Krull dimension one, and the maximal ideal of R is principal.
5. R is an integrally closed noetherian local ring with Krull dimension one.
6. R is a unique factorization domain with a unique irreducible element (up to multiplication with units.)
7. R is local, not a field, and every nonzero fractional ideal of R is irreducible.
8. There is some Dedekind valuation v on the field of fractions K of R, such that R={x : x in K, v(x) ≥ 0}.

Let $Z_{(2)}$={ p/q : p, q in Z, q odd }. Then the field of fractions of $Z_{(2)}$ is Q. Now, for any nonzero element r of Q, we can apply unique factorization to the numerator and denominator of r to write r as $2^k p/q$, where p, q, and k are integers with p and q odd. In this case, we define v(r)=k.

- a. Localization of a category
- b. Discrete valuation ring
- c. Localization of a module
- d. Localized

14. In algebra (in particular in algebraic geometry or algebraic number theory), a _____ is a function on a field that provides a measure of size or multiplicity of elements of the field. They generalize to commutative algebra the notion of size inherent in consideration of the degree of a pole or multiplicity of a zero in complex analysis, the degree divisibility of a number by a prime number in number theory, and the geometrical concept of contact between two algebraic or analytic varieties in algebraic geometry.

A field with a _____ on it is called a valued field.

- a. Stable vector bundle
- b. Valuation
- c. Motivic integration
- d. Pencil

15. In abstract algebra, a _____ is an integral domain D such that for every element x of its field of fractions F, at least one of x or x^{-1} belongs to D.

Given a field F, if D is a subring of F such that either x or x^{-1} belongs to D for every x in F, then D is said to be a _____ for the field F. Since F is in this case indeed the field of fractions of D, a _____ for a field is a _____. Another way to characterize the valuation rings of a field F is that valuation rings D of F have F as their field of fractions, and their ideals are totally ordered by inclusion; or equivalently their principal ideals are totally ordered by inclusion.

- a. Near-field
- b. Rupture field
- c. Valuation ring
- d. Left alternative

16. In algebraic geometry, divisors are a generalization of codimension one subvarieties of algebraic varieties; two different generalizations are in common use, Cartier divisors and Weil divisors The concepts agree on non-singular varieties over algebraically closed fields.

A Weil _____ is a locally finite linear combination (with integral coefficients) of irreducible subvarieties of codimension one.

- a. Divisor
- b. Picard group
- c. Lefschetz pencil
- d. Linear system of divisors

17. In algebra, the _____ of a polynomial is the highest common factor of its coefficients.

A polynomial is primitive if it has _____ unity.

Gauss's lemma for polynomials may be expressed as stating that for polynomials over a unique factorization domain, the _____ of the product of two polynomials is the product of their contents.

a. Filtration
b. Nested radical
c. Content
d. Permanent

18. In field theory, a branch of mathematics, a _____ is the minimal polynomial of a primitive element of the finite extension field GF(p^m.) In other words, a polynomial F(X) with coefficients in GF(p) = Z/pZ is a _____ if it has a root α in GF(p^m) such that $\{0, 1, \alpha, \alpha^2, \alpha^3, \ldots, \alpha^{p^m-2}\}$ is the entire field GF(p^m), and moreover, F(X) is the smallest degree polynomial having α as root.

In ring theory, the term _____ is used for a different purpose, to mean a polynomial over a unique factorization domain (such as the integers) whose greatest common divisor of its coefficients is a unit.

a. Primitive polynomial
b. Separable
c. Kummer theory
d. Formally real field

19. In algebra, the nth _____, for any positive integer n, is the monic polynomial

where the product is over all primitive n^{th} roots of unity ω, i.e. all the complex numbers ω of order n.

The degree of Φ_n, or in other words the number of factors in its definition above, is φ(n), where φ is Euler's totient function.

The coefficients of Φ_n are integers.

a. Cyclic number
b. Q-Vandermonde identity
c. Cyclotomic polynomial
d. Character group

20. This article deals with the ring of complex numbers integral over Z. For the general notion of _____, see Integrality.

In number theory, an _____ is a complex number that is a root of some monic polynomial (leading coefficient 1) with coefficients in Z. The set of all algebraic integers is closed under addition and multiplication and therefore is a subring of complex numbers denoted by A. The ring A is the integral closure of regular integers Z in complex numbers.

The ring of integers of a number field K, denoted by O_K, is the intersection of K and A: it can also be characterised as the maximal order of the field K. Each _____ belongs to the ring of integers of some number field.

Chapter 6. Commutative Rings II

a. Algebraic integer
b. Adele ring
c. Additive polynomial
d. Algebraic number theory

21. In algebra, a _____ of an element in a quadratic extension field of a field K is its image under the unique non-identity automorphism of the extended field that fixes K. If the extension is generated by a square root of an element r of K, then the _____ of $a + b\sqrt{r}$ is $a - b\sqrt{r}$ for $a, b \in K$, and in particular in the case of the field C of complex numbers as an extension of the field R of real numbers (where r = − 1), the complex _____ of a + bi is a − bi.

Forming the sum or product of any element of the extension field with its _____ always gives an element of K. This can be used to rewrite a quotient of numbers in the extended field so that the denominator lies in K, by multiplying numerator and denominator by the _____ of the denominator. This process is called rationalization of the denominator, in particular if K is the field Q of rational numbers.

a. Digital root
b. K-theory
c. Field arithmetic
d. Conjugate

22. The _____ are natural numbers including 0 ' href='/wiki/0_(number)'>0, 1, 2, 3, ...) and their negatives (0, −1, −2, −3, ...). They are numbers that can be written without a fractional or decimal component, and fall within the set {...

a. Integers
b. ADE classification
c. Abelian P-root group
d. AKS primality test

23. In field theory, given a field extension E / F and an element α of E which is an algebraic element over F, the _____ of α is the monic polynomial p, with coefficients in F, of least degree such that p(α) = 0. The _____ is irreducible over F, and any other non-zero polynomial f with f(α) = 0 is a (polynomial) multiple of p.

For example, for $F = \mathbb{Q}, E = \mathbb{R}, \alpha = \sqrt{2}$ the _____ for α is p(x) = x² − 2.

a. Vandermonde polynomial
b. Minimal polynomial
c. Ring of symmetric functions
d. Kazhdan-Lusztig polynomials

24. The _____ and descending chain condition (DCC) are finiteness properties satisfied by certain algebraic structures, most importantly, ideals in a commutative ring. These conditions played an important role in the development of the structure theory of commutative rings in the works of David Hilbert, Emmy Noether, and Emil Artin. The conditions themselves can be stated in an abstract form, so that they make sense for any partially ordered set.

a. Ascending chain condition
b. Integral
c. Invariant polynomial
d. Atomic domain

25. In algebraic topology, a simplicial k-_____ is a formal linear combination of k-simplices.

Integration is defined on chains by taking the linear combination of integrals over the simplices in the _____ with coefficients typically integers. The set of all k-chains forms a group and the sequence of these groups is called a _____ complex.

Chapter 6. Commutative Rings II

a. Combinatorial topology
b. Bockstein homomorphism
c. Chain
d. Tesseract

26. In linear algebra, a _____ is a set of vectors that, in a linear combination, can represent every vector in a given vector space or free module, and such that no element of the set can be represented as a linear combination of the others. In other words, a _____ is a linearly independent spanning set.
    a. Chirality
    b. Supergroup
    c. Basis
    d. Minor

27. In mathematics, an _____ is an isomorphism from a mathematical object to itself. It is, in some sense, a symmetry of the object, and a way of mapping the object to itself while preserving all of its structure. The set of all automorphisms of an object forms a group, called the _____ group.
    a. Endomorphism
    b. ADE classification
    c. Automorphism
    d. Epimorphism

28. In abstract algebra, a _____ is an algebraic structure with notions of addition, subtraction, multiplication and division, satisfying certain axioms. The most commonly used fields are the _____ of real numbers, the _____ of complex numbers, and the _____ of rational numbers, but there are also finite fields, fields of functions, various algebraic number fields, p-adic fields, and so forth.

Any _____ may be used as the scalars for a vector space, which is the standard general context for linear algebra.

    a. Field
    b. Generic polynomial
    c. Separable
    d. Tensor product of fields

29. In abstract algebra, the concept of a _____ over a ring is a generalization of the notion of vector space, where instead of requiring the scalars to lie in a field, the 'scalars' may lie in an arbitrary ring. Modules also generalize the notion of abelian groups, which are modules over $\mathbb{Z}$.

Thus, a _____, like a vector space, is an additive abelian group; a product is defined between elements of the ring and elements of the _____, and this multiplication is associative (when used with the multiplication in the ring) and distributive.

    a. Goodman-Nguyen-van Fraassen algebra
    b. Semigroupoid
    c. Near-field
    d. Module

30. In mathematics, particularly abstract algebra, an _____ of a field K is an algebraic extension of K that is algebraically closed. It is one of many closures in mathematics.

Using Zorn's lemma, it can be shown that every field has an _____, and that the _____ of a field K is unique up to an isomorphism that fixes every member of K. Because of this essential uniqueness, we often speak of the _____ of K, rather than an _____ of K.

a. Algebraic extension
c. Algebraic closure
b. Archimedean property
d. Adjunction

31. In mathematics, a field F is said to be _____ if every polynomial in one variable of degree at least 1, with coefficients in F, has a root in F.

As an example, the field of real numbers is not _____, because the polynomial equation $x^2 + 1 = 0$ has no solution in real numbers, even though all its coefficients (1 and 0) are real. The same argument proves that no subfield of the real field is _____; in particular, the field of rational numbers is not _____.

a. Inverse semigroup
c. Unique factorization domain
b. Ordered exponential
d. Algebraically closed

32. In mathematics, the _____ construction in abstract algebra constructs an abelian group from a commutative monoid in the best possible way. It takes its name from the more general construction in category theory, introduced by Alexander Grothendieck in his fundamental work of the mid-1950s that resulted in the development of K-theory. The _____ is denoted by K or K_0.

a. Restriction of scalars
c. Power set
b. Grothendieck group
d. Coimage

33. A _____ is a set G closed under a binary operation · satisfying the following 3 axioms:

- Associativity: For all a, b and c in G, (a · b) · c = a · (b · c.)
- Identity element: There exists an e∈G such that for all a in G, e · a = a · e = a.
- Inverse element: For each a in G, there is an element b in G such that a · b = b · a = e, where e is an identity element.

Basic examples for groups are the integers Z with addition operation, or rational numbers without zero Q{0} with multiplication. More generally, for any ring R, the units in R form a multiplicative _____ Groups include, however, much more general structures than the above.

a. Grigorchuk group
c. Nilpotent group
b. Product of group subsets
d. Group

34. In mathematics, there are several meanings of _____ depending on the subject.

A _____, usually denoted by ° (the _____ symbol), is a measurement of plane angle, representing $1/360$ of a full rotation. When that angle is with respect to a reference meridian, it indicates a location along a great circle of a sphere, such as Earth , Mars, or the celestial sphere.

a. Relation algebra
c. Median algebra
b. Symmetric difference
d. Degree

Chapter 6. Commutative Rings II

35. In mathematics, a _____ is any function which can be written as the ratio of two polynomial functions. _____ of degree 2 : $y = \dfrac{x^2 - 3x - 2}{x^2 - 4}$

In the case of one variable, x, a _____ is a function of the form

$$f(x) = \frac{P(x)}{Q(x)}$$

where P and Q are polynomial function in x and Q is not the zero polynomial. The domain of f is the set of all points x for which the denominator Q(x) is not zero.

- a. -module
- b. Legendre rational functions
- c. -equivalence
- d. Rational function

36. In mathematics, the term _____ is used to describe an algebraic structures which in some sense cannot be divided by a smaller structure of the same type. Put another way, an algebraic structure is _____ if the kernel of every homomorphism is either the whole structure or a single element. Some examples are:

- A group is called a _____ group if it does not contain a non-trivial proper normal subgroup.
- A ring is called a _____ ring if it does not contain a non-trivial two sided ideal.
- A module is called a _____ module if does not contain a non-trivial submodule.
- An algebra is called a _____ algebra if does not contain a non-trivial two sided ideal.

The general pattern is that the structure admits no non-trivial congruence relations.

- a. Commutativity
- b. Polarization identity
- c. Linear combinations
- d. Simple

37. A _____ is a symbol that stands for a value that may vary; the term usually occurs in opposition to constant, which is a symbol for a non-varying value, i.e. completely fixed or fixed in the context of use. The concepts of constants and variables are fundamental to all modern mathematics, science, engineering, and computer programming.

Much of the basic theory for which we use variables today, such as school geometry and algebra, was developed thousands of years ago, but the use of symbolic formulae and variables is only several hundreds of years old.

- a. 2-bridge knot
- b. -module
- c. -equivalence
- d. Variable

38. In abstract algebra, a subset S of a field L is _____ over a subfield K if the elements of S do not satisfy any non-trivial polynomial equation with coefficients in K. This means that for every finite sequence $a_1, ..., a_n$ of elements of S, no two the same, and every non-zero polynomial $P(x_1, ..., x_n)$ with coefficients in K, we have

$P(a_1,...,a_n) \neq 0$.

In particular, a one element set {α} is _____ over K if and only if α is transcendental over K. In general, all the elements of an _____ set over K are by necessity transcendental over K, but that is far from being a sufficient condition.

For example, the subset {√π, 2π+1} of the real numbers R is not _____ over the rational numbers Q, since the non-zero polynomial

$$P(x_1, x_2) = 2x_1^2 - x_2 + 1$$

yields zero when √π is substituted for x_1 and 2π+1 is substituted for x_2.

   a. Expression
   c. Unital
   b. Involution
   d. Algebraically independent

39. In mathematics, the _____ of a ring R, often denoted char(R), is defined to be the smallest number of times one must add the ring's multiplicative identity element (1) to itself to get the additive identity element (0); the ring is said to have _____ zero if this repeated sum never reaches the additive identity. That is, char(R) is the smallest positive number n such that

$$\underbrace{1 + \cdots + 1}_{n \text{ summands}} = 0$$

if such a number n exists, and 0 otherwise. The _____ may also be taken to be the exponent of the ring's additive group, that is, the smallest positive n such that

$$\underbrace{a + \cdots + a}_{n \text{ summands}} = 0$$

for every element a of the ring (again, if n exists; otherwise zero.)

   a. Coherent ring
   c. Characteristic
   b. Free ideal ring
   d. Hereditary

40. In algebraic geometry, the _____ of an algebraic variety V consists of objects which are interpreted as rational functions on V. In complex algebraic geometry these are meromorphic functions and their higher-dimensional analogues; in classical algebraic geometry they are ratios of polynomials; in modern algebraic geometry they are elements of some quotient field.

More precisely, in complex algebraic geometry the objects of study are complex analytic varieties, on which we have a local notion of complex analysis, through which we may define meromorphic functions. The _____ is then the set of all meromorphic functions on the variety.

a. Local zeta-function
b. Zariski surface
c. Segre embedding
d. Function field

41. In abstract algebra, the _____ of a field extension L / K is a certain rather coarse measure of the 'size' of the extension. Specifically, it is defined as the largest cardinality of an algebraically independent subset of L over K.

A subset S of L is a transcendence basis of L / K if it is algebraically independent over K and if furthermore L is an algebraic extension of the field K(S) (the field obtained by adjoining the elements of S to K.)

a. Primitive polynomial
b. Field extension
c. Splitting field
d. Transcendence degree

42. In mathematics, especially in the area of algebra known as commutative algebra, certain prime ideals called _____ ideals play an important role in understanding rings and modules. The notion of height and Krull's Hauptidealsatz use minimal primes.

A prime ideal P is said to be a _____ ideal over an ideal I if there are no prime ideals strictly contained in P that contain I. A prime ideal is said to be a _____ ideal if it is a _____ ideal over the zero ideal.

a. Gorenstein ring
b. Minimal prime
c. Noether normalization lemma
d. Divided power structure

43. In mathematics, a polynomial P(X) is _____ over a field K if all of its irreducible factors have distinct roots in an algebraic closure of K - that is each irreducible factor of P(X) has distinct linear factors in some large enough field extension. There is, however, another, non-equivalent definition of separability. It says that P is _____ if and only if it is coprime to its formal derivative P'.

a. Global field
b. Separable
c. Field of fractions
d. Transcendence degree

44. In mathematics, namely algebraic geometry, the _____ is a particular topology chosen for algebraic varieties that reflects the algebraic nature of their definition. It is due to Oscar Zariski and took a place of particular importance in the field around 1950. Joe Harris says in his introductory lectures that it is 'not a real topology' and points out that in the _____, every two algebraic curves are homeomorphic simply because their underlying sets have equal cardinalities and their topologies are both cofinite.

a. Theorem of the cube
b. Degree of an algebraic variety
c. Segre embedding
d. Zariski topology

45. In geometry, a _____ is a generalization of the concept of hyperplane. Suppose an enveloping manifold M has n dimensions; then any submanifold of M of n − 1 dimensions is a _____. Equivalently, the codimension of a _____ is one.

a. Shimura variety
b. Chow coordinates
c. Direction cosines
d. Hypersurface

46. In mathematics, an element x of a ring R is called _____ if there exists some positive integer n such that $x^n = 0$.

The term was introduced by Benjamin Peirce in the context of elements of an algebra that vanish when raised to a power.

- This definition can be applied in particular to square matrices. The matrix

$$A = \begin{pmatrix} 0 & 1 & 0 \\ 0 & 0 & 1 \\ 0 & 0 & 0 \end{pmatrix}$$

is _____ because $A^3 = 0$. See _____ matrix for more.

a. Ring of integers
b. Nilpotent
c. Hochschild homology
d. Product ring

47. In ring theory, a branch of abstract algebra, a _____ is an ideal I in a ring R that is generated by a single element a of R.

More specifically:

- a left _____ of R is a subset of R of the form Ra := {ra : r in R};
- a right _____ is a subset of the form aR := {ar : r in R};
- a two-sided _____ is a subset of the form RaR := {$r_1 a s_1$ + ... + $r_n a s_n$: $r_1, s_1, ..., r_n, s_n$ in R}.

If R is a commutative ring, then the above three notions are all the same. In that case, it is common to write the ideal generated by a as (a.)

Not all ideals are principal.

a. Primitive ideal
b. Radical of an ideal
c. Radical of an ring
d. Principal ideal

48. In abstract algebra, a _____ i.e., can be generated by a single element. More generally, a principal ring is a nonzero commutative ring whose ideals are principal, although some authors (e.g., Bourbaki) refers to Principal ideal domains as principal rings. The distinction being that a principal ideal ring may have zero divisors whereas a _____ cannot.

a. Principal ideal domain
b. Discrete valuation
c. Nilradical
d. Minimal prime

49. The _____ of a Lie algebra 𝔤 is a particular ideal of 𝔤.

Chapter 6. Commutative Rings II

Let 𝔤 be a Lie algebra. The _____ of 𝔤 is defined as the largest solvable ideal of 𝔤.

a. Cyclically reduced word
b. Radical
c. Garside element
d. Class sum

50. In ring theory, a commutative ring R is called a _____ if it has no non-zero nilpotent elements. A commutative algebra over a commutative ring is called a reduced algebra if its underlying ring is reduced.

The nilpotent elements of a commutative ring A form an ideal of A, the so-called nilradical or nilpotent radical of A; therefore a commutative ring is reduced if and only if its nilpotent radical is reduced to zero.

a. Jaffard ring
b. Regular p-group
c. Cyclically reduced word
d. Reduced ring

51. In mathematics, the adjective _____ means that an object cannot be expressed as a product of more than one non-trivial factors in a given set. See also factorization.

For any field F, the ring of polynomials with coefficients in F is denoted by F[x].

a. Ehrhart polynomial
b. Integer-valued polynomial
c. Alternating polynomial
d. Irreducible

52. In set theory, the term _____ refers to a set operation used in the convergence of set elements to form a resultant set containing the elements of both sets. As a simple example, a _____ of two disjoint sets, which do not have elements in common results in a set containing all elements from both sets. A Venn diagram representing the _____ of sets A and B. If one circle represents A, and the other B, then the red area represents the _____ of A and B. The area where the circles join, also shown in red, is the intersection of the two sets.

If we define two sets which contain unique elements; those of A not occurring in B and vice versa, then the _____ of these sets results in a set which contains all elements of A and B. In terms of notation, we could define this set operation as the following:

A = {1,2,3,4}
B = {5,6,7,8}
$$A \cup B = \{1, 2, 3, 4, 5, 6, 7, 8\}$$

Other more complex operations can be done including the _____, if the set is for example defined by a property rather than a finite or assumed infinite enumeration of elements.

a. ADE classification
b. Abelian P-root group
c. AKS primality test
d. Union

53. For example, in Z, (p^n) is a _____ if p is a prime number.

The notion of primary ideals is important in commutative ring theory because every noetherian ring has a primary decomposition: that is, an ideal can be written as an intersection of finitely many primary ideals. (This result is known as Lasker-Noether theorem.)

- a. Mukai-Fourier transform
- b. Parametrix
- c. S plane
- d. Primary ideal

54. In mathematics, an _____ of a module M over a commutative ring R is a prime ideal of R that is the annihilator of some element of M.

A module is called coprimary if xm = 0 for some nonzero m ∈ M implies x^nM = 0 for some positive integer n. A finitely generated module over a Noetherian ring is coprimary if and only if it has at most one _____.

- a. Invariant polynomial
- b. Integral
- c. Atomic domain
- d. Associated prime

55. In algebra, the _____ of a commutative ring is a nilpotent ideal, which is as large as possible. In the non-commutative ring case, more care is needed resulting in several related radicals.

The _____ of a commutative ring is the set of all nilpotent elements in the ring, or equivalently the radical of the zero ideal.

- a. Top
- b. Hilbert polynomial
- c. Noether normalization lemma
- d. Nilradical

56. In mathematics, the word _____ means two different things in the context of polynomials:

- The first meaning is a product of powers of variables, or formally any value obtained from 1 by finitely many multiplications by a variable. If only a single variable x is considered this means that any _____ is either 1 or a power x^n of x, with n a positive integer. If several variables are considered, say, x, y, z, then each can be given an exponent, so that any _____ is of the form $x^a y^b z^c$ with a,b,c nonnegative integers (taking note that any exponent 0 makes the corresponding factor equal to 1.)
- The second meaning of _____ includes monomials in the first sense, but also allows multiplication by any constant, so that $-7x^5$ and $(3 - 4i)x^4 yz^{13}$ are also considered to be monomials (the second example assuming polynomials in x, y, z over the complex numbers are considered.)

With either definition, the set of monomials is a subset of all polynomials that is closed under multiplication.

Both uses of this notion can be found, and in many cases the distinction is simply ignored, see for instance examples for the first and second meaning, and an unclear definition. In informal discussions the distinction is seldom important, and tendency is towards the broader second meaning. When studying the structure of polynomials however, one often definitely needs a notion with the first meaning.

a. Schur polynomials
c. Power sum symmetric polynomial
b. Diagonal form
d. Monomial

57. In mathematics, a _____ is a total order on the set of all monomials (considering monomials which only differ in their coefficient to be the same) satisfying two additional properties.

   1. If u < v and w is any other monomial, then uw<vw. In other words, the ordering respects multiplication.
   2. The ordering is a well ordering

Most monomial orders impose an ordering on the indeterminates, but differ in their exact details. Some important examples of monomial orders include:

- Lexicographic order (lex) orders according to the highest power of the most significant indeterminate, using less significant indeterminates to break ties.

- Reverse lexicographic order (revlex) orders according to the lowest power of the least significant indeterminate, using more significant indeterminates to break ties.

- Graded lexicographic order (grlex) orders by total degree first, then breaks ties using lexicographic order.

- Graded reverse lexicographic order (grevlex) orders by total degree first, then breaks ties using reverse lexicographic order.

- An elimination order guarantees that a monomial involving any of a set of indeterminates will always be greater than a monomial not involving any of them.

- A product order orders one set of indeterminates using one _____, then breaks ties using a different order on a second set.

- Weight orders treat the powers of indeterminates as a vector and orders according to the dot product with a weight vector.

All monomial orders can be constructed as product orders of weight orders (Cox et al. pp.

a. -module
c. 2-bridge knot
b. -equivalence
d. Monomial order

58. In group theory, a branch of mathematics, the term _____ is used in two closely related senses:

- the _____ of a group is its cardinality, i.e. the number of its elements;
- the _____, sometimes period, of an element a of a group is the smallest positive integer m such that a^m = e (where e denotes the identity element of the group, and a^m denotes the product of m copies of a.) If no such m exists, we say that a has infinite _____. All elements of finite groups have finite _____.

Chapter 6. Commutative Rings II

We denote the _____ of a group G by ord(G) or $|G|$ and the _____ of an element a by ord(a) or $|a|$.

Example. The symmetric group S_3 has the following multiplication table.

This group has six elements, so ord(S_3) = 6.

- a. Outer automorphism group
- b. Artin group
- c. Order
- d. Index calculus algorithm

59. In mathematics, _____ refers to the rewriting of an expression into a simpler form. For example, the process of rewriting a fraction into one with the smallest whole-number denominator possible (while keeping the numerator an integer) is called 'reducing a fraction'. Rewriting a radical (or 'root') expression with the smallest possible whole number under the radical symbol is called 'reducing a radical'.

- a. 2-bridge knot
- b. Reduction
- c. -equivalence
- d. -module

Chapter 7. Modules and Categories

1. A _____ between two algebras over a field K, A and B, is a map $F : A \to B$ such that for all k in K and x,y in A,

   - F(kx) = kF(x)

   - F(x + y) = F(x) + F(y)

   - F(xy) = F(x)F(y)

   If F is bijective then F is said to be an isomorphism between A and B.

   Let A = K[x] be the set of all polynomials over a field K and B be the set of all polynomial functions over K. Both A and B are algebras over K given by the standard multiplication and addition of polynomials and functions, respectively. We can map each f in A to $\hat{f}$ in B by the rule $\hat{f}(t) = f(t)$. A routine check shows that the mapping $f \mapsto \hat{f}$ is a _____ of the algebras A and B. If K is a finite field then let

   $$p(x) = \Pi_{t \in K}(x - t).$$

   p is a nonzero polynomial in K[x], however $p(t) = 0$ for all t in K, so $\hat{p} = 0$ is the zero function and the algebras are not isomorphic.

   a. Frobenius matrix
   b. Tensor algebra
   c. Tensor product of algebras
   d. Homomorphism

2. In abstract algebra, an _____ is a bijective map f such that both f and its inverse f^{-1} are homomorphisms, i.e., structure-preserving mappings. In the more general setting of category theory, an _____ is a morphism f:X→Y in a category for which there exists an 'inverse' f^{-1}:Y→X, with the property that both $f^{-1}f$=id$_X$ and ff^{-1}=id$_Y$.

   Informally, an _____ is a kind of mapping between objects, which shows a relationship between two properties or operations.

   a. Epimorphism
   b. Endomorphism
   c. ADE classification
   d. Isomorphism

3. In abstract algebra, the concept of a _____ over a ring is a generalization of the notion of vector space, where instead of requiring the scalars to lie in a field, the 'scalars' may lie in an arbitrary ring. Modules also generalize the notion of abelian groups, which are modules over $\mathbb{Z}$.

   Thus, a _____, like a vector space, is an additive abelian group; a product is defined between elements of the ring and elements of the _____, and this multiplication is associative (when used with the multiplication in the ring) and distributive.

   a. Goodman-Nguyen-van Fraassen algebra
   b. Semigroupoid
   c. Near-field
   d. Module

4. In mathematics, especially in the area of abstract algebra known as ring theory, a _____ is a ring with 0 ≠ 1 such that ab = 0 implies that either a = 0 or b = 0 (the zero-product property.) That is, it is a nontrivial ring without left or right zero divisors. A commutative _____ is called an integral _____.

   a. Coherent ring
   b. Subring
   c. Domain
   d. Partially-ordered ring

5. In mathematics, any vector space, V, has a corresponding dual vector space (or just dual space for short) consisting of all linear functionals on V. Dual vector spaces defined on finite-dimensional vector spaces can be used for defining tensors which are studied in tensor algebra. When applied to vector spaces of functions (which typically are infinite-dimensional), _____ are employed for defining and studying concepts like measures, distributions, and Hilbert spaces. Consequently, the dual space is an important concept in the study of functional analysis.

   a. Barycentric coordinates
   b. Jordan normal form
   c. Conjugate transpose
   d. Dual spaces

6. In ring theory, a branch of abstract algebra, an _____ is a special subset of a ring. The _____ concept generalizes in an appropriate way some important properties of integers like 'even number' or 'multiple of 3'.

For instance, in rings one studies prime ideals instead of prime numbers, one defines coprime ideals as a generalization of coprime numbers, and one can prove a generalized Chinese remainder theorem about ideals.

   a. AKS primality test
   b. ADE classification
   c. Augmentation ideal
   d. Ideal

7. In linear algebra, a branch of mathematics, a _____ or linear form is a linear map from a vector space to its field of scalars. In R^n, if vectors are represented as column vectors, then linear functionals are represented as row vectors, and their action on vectors given by the matrix product. In general, if V is a vector space over a field k, then a _____ f is a function from V to k which is linear:

$$f(\vec{v} + \vec{w}) = f(\vec{v}) + f(\vec{w}) \text{ for all } \vec{v}, \vec{w} \in V$$
$$f(a\vec{v}) = af(\vec{v}) \text{ for all } \vec{v} \in V, a \in k$$

The set of all linear functionals from V to k, Hom_k, is itself a vector space over k.

   a. Cofactor
   b. Change of bases
   c. Generalized Pauli matrices
   d. Linear functional

8. In ring theory, a branch of abstract algebra, a _____ is an ideal I in a ring R that is generated by a single element a of R.

Chapter 7. Modules and Categories

More specifically:

- a left _____ of R is a subset of R of the form Ra := {ra : r in R};
- a right _____ is a subset of the form aR := {ar : r in R};
- a two-sided _____ is a subset of the form RaR := {$r_1 a s_1 + ... + r_n a s_n$: $r_1, s_1, ..., r_n, s_n$ in R}.

If R is a commutative ring, then the above three notions are all the same. In that case, it is common to write the ideal generated by a as (a.)

Not all ideals are principal.

a. Radical of an ring
c. Principal ideal

b. Radical of an ideal
d. Primitive ideal

9. In abstract algebra, a _____ i.e., can be generated by a single element. More generally, a principal ring is a nonzero commutative ring whose ideals are principal, although some authors (e.g., Bourbaki) refers to Principal ideal domains as principal rings. The distinction being that a principal ideal ring may have zero divisors whereas a _____ cannot.

a. Nilradical
c. Principal ideal domain

b. Discrete valuation
d. Minimal prime

10. In mathematics, more specifically in ring theory, a _____ is a module over a ring which is generated by one element. The term is by analogy with cyclic groups, that is groups which are generated by one element.

A left R-module M is called cyclic if M can be generated by a single element i.e. M = (x) = R x = {rx | r ∈ R} for some x in M. Similarly, a right R-module N is cyclic, if N = y R for some y ∈ N.

a. Ring extension
c. Superalgebra

b. Semisimple
d. Cyclic module

11. In mathematics, a _____ is a module that has a finite generating set. Equivalently, it is a homomorphic image of a free module on finitely many generators. The kernel of this homomorphism need not be finitely generated (then the module is finitely presented); over a Noetherian ring both concepts coincide.

a. Tensor product of modules
c. Relative tensor product

b. Morita equivalence
d. Finitely generated module

12. In mathematics, an _____ of a linear mapping

$$T : V \to V$$

from some vector space V to itself is a subspace W of V such that T(W) is contained in W. An _____ of T is also said to be T invariant.

If W is T-invariant, we can restrict T to W to arrive at a new linear mapping

   T|W : W → W.

Next we give a few immediate examples of invariant subspaces.

- a. Orthogonal Procrustes problem
- b. Invariant subspace
- c. Orthogonal complement
- d. Indeterminate system

13. In mathematics, _____ are a concept central to linear algebra and related fields of mathematics

Suppose that K is a field and V is a vector space over K. As usual, we call elements of V vectors and call elements of K scalars.

- a. Left alternative
- b. Linear combinations
- c. Hyperstructures
- d. Groupoid

14. In mathematics, a _____ is an algebraic structure whose main use is in studying geometric objects such as Lie groups and differentiable manifolds. Lie algebras were introduced to study the concept of infinitesimal transformations. The term '_____') was introduced by Hermann Weyl in the 1930s.
- a. Lorentz group
- b. Weyl group
- c. Maximal torus
- d. Lie algebra

15. A _____ is a left or right _____ of some subgroup in G. Since Hg = g(g^{-1}Hg), the right cosets Hg (of H) and the left cosets g(g^{-1}Hg) (of the conjugate subgroup g^{-1}Hg) are the same. Hence it is not meaningful to speak of a _____ as being left or right unless one first specifies the underlying subgroup.

For abelian groups or groups written additively, the notation used changes to g+H and H+g respectively.

- a. Coset
- b. Burnside ring
- c. Wreath product
- d. Grigorchuk group

16. In mathematics, the term _____ is used to describe an algebraic structures which in some sense cannot be divided by a smaller structure of the same type. Put another way, an algebraic structure is _____ if the kernel of every homomorphism is either the whole structure or a single element. Some examples are:

- A group is called a _____ group if it does not contain a non-trivial proper normal subgroup.
- A ring is called a _____ ring if it does not contain a non-trivial two sided ideal.
- A module is called a _____ module if does not contain a non-trivial submodule.
- An algebra is called a _____ algebra if does not contain a non-trivial two sided ideal.

The general pattern is that the structure admits no non-trivial congruence relations.

Chapter 7. Modules and Categories

a. Linear combinations
c. Simple
b. Polarization identity
d. Commutativity

17. In abstract algebra, a (left or right) module S over a ring R is called simple or irreducible if it is not the zero module 0 and if its only submodules are 0 and S. Understanding the _____ over a ring is usually helpful because these modules form the 'building blocks' of all other modules in a certain sense.

Abelian groups are the same as Z-modules. The simple Z-modules are precisely the cyclic groups of prime order.

a. Semisimple module
c. Tensor product of modules
b. Socle
d. Simple modules

18. In abstract algebra, the _____ is a construction which combines several modules into a new, larger module. The result of the direct summation of modules is the 'smallest general' module which contains the given modules as subspaces. This is an example of a coproduct.

a. Finite dimensional von Neumann algebra
c. Schmidt decomposition
b. Frame
d. Direct sum

19. The term _____ is useful for describing certain algebraic structures. The term comes from the concept of an _____ binary operation which is a binary operation that draws from some _____ set. To be more specific, a left _____ binary operation on S over R is a function $f : R \times S \to S$ and a right _____ binary operation on S over R is a function $f : S \times R \to S$ where S is the set the operation is defined on, and R is the _____ set (the set the operation is defined over.)

a. Orthogonal
c. Unit ring
b. Algebraic structure
d. External

20. In mathematics, the _____ of a ring R, often denoted char(R), is defined to be the smallest number of times one must add the ring's multiplicative identity element (1) to itself to get the additive identity element (0); the ring is said to have _____ zero if this repeated sum never reaches the additive identity. That is, char(R) is the smallest positive number n such that

$$\underbrace{1 + \cdots + 1}_{n \text{ summands}} = 0$$

if such a number n exists, and 0 otherwise. The _____ may also be taken to be the exponent of the ring's additive group, that is, the smallest positive n such that

$$\underbrace{a + \cdots + a}_{n \text{ summands}} = 0$$

for every element a of the ring (again, if n exists; otherwise zero.)

a. Free ideal ring
c. Coherent ring
b. Hereditary
d. Characteristic

Chapter 7. Modules and Categories

21. This article deals with the ring of complex numbers integral over Z. For the general notion of _____, see Integrality.

In number theory, an _____ is a complex number that is a root of some monic polynomial (leading coefficient 1) with coefficients in Z. The set of all algebraic integers is closed under addition and multiplication and therefore is a subring of complex numbers denoted by A. The ring A is the integral closure of regular integers Z in complex numbers.

The ring of integers of a number field K, denoted by O_K, is the intersection of K and A: it can also be characterised as the maximal order of the field K. Each _____ belongs to the ring of integers of some number field.

- a. Adele ring
- b. Algebraic number theory
- c. Additive polynomial
- d. Algebraic integer

22. The _____ are natural numbers including 0 ' href='/wiki/0_(number)'>0, 1, 2, 3, ...) and their negatives (0, −1, −2, −3, ...). They are numbers that can be written without a fractional or decimal component, and fall within the set {...

- a. AKS primality test
- b. ADE classification
- c. Abelian P-root group
- d. Integers

23. In mathematics, the _____ of a linear mapping of vector spaces f : X → Y is the quotient space Y/im(f) of the codomain of f by the image of f.

Cokernels are dual to the kernels of category theory, hence the name: the kernel is a subobject of the domain (it maps to the domain), while the _____ is a quotient object of the codomain (it maps from the codomain.)

Intuitively, given an equation f(x) = y that one is seeking to solve, the _____ measures the constraints that y must satisfy for this equation to have a solution - the obstructions to a solution - while the kernel measures the degrees of freedom in a solution, if one exists.

- a. Cokernel
- b. Distributivity
- c. BCK algebras
- d. Normal extension

24. In mathematics, _____ is an invariant of knots and links that arises as the homology of a chain complex. It may be regarded as a categorification of the Jones polynomial.

It was developed in the late 1990s by Mikhail Khovanov, then at the University of California, Davis, now at Columbia University.

- a. Cellular homology
- b. Homology theory
- c. Homology
- d. Khovanov homology

Chapter 7. Modules and Categories

25. In mathematics, _____ or factoring is the decomposition of an object ' href='/wiki/Matrix_(mathematics)'>matrix) into a product of other objects, or factors, which when multiplied together give the original. For example, the number 15 factors into primes as 3 × 5, and the polynomial $x^2 - 4$ factors as $(x - 2)(x + 2)$. In all cases, a product of simpler objects is obtained.
   a. 2-bridge knot
   b. -module
   c. -equivalence
   d. Factorization

26. In mathematics, a _____ is an abstraction derived from structure-preserving mappings between two mathematical structures.

The study of morphisms and of the structures (called objects) over which they are defined, is central to category theory. Much of the terminology of morphisms, as well as the intuition underlying them, comes from concrete categories, where the objects are simply sets with some additional structure, and morphisms are functions preserving this structure.

   a. Rotation
   b. Linear map
   c. Reflection
   d. Morphism

27. In mathematics, a _____ is, roughly speaking, a commutative ring in which every element, with special exceptions, can be uniquely written as a product of prime elements, analogous to the fundamental theorem of arithmetic for the integers. Unique factorization domains are sometimes called factorial rings, following the terminology of Bourbaki.

Note that unique factorization domains appear in the following chain of class inclusions:

- Commutative rings >⊃ integral domains >⊃ unique factorization domains >⊃ principal ideal domains >⊃ Euclidean domains >⊃ fields

   a. Unique factorization domain
   b. Isomorphism class
   c. Unit ring
   d. Absorption law

28. In set theory, the term _____ refers to a set operation used in the convergence of set elements to form a resultant set containing the elements of both sets. As a simple example, a _____ of two disjoint sets, which do not have elements in common results in a set containing all elements from both sets. A Venn diagram representing the _____ of sets A and B. If one circle represents A, and the other B, then the red area represents the _____ of A and B. The area where the circles join, also shown in red, is the intersection of the two sets.

If we define two sets which contain unique elements; those of A not occurring in B and vice versa, then the _____ of these sets results in a set which contains all elements of A and B. In terms of notation, we could define this set operation as the following:

A = {1,2,3,4}
B = {5,6,7,8}
$$A \cup B = \{1, 2, 3, 4, 5, 6, 7, 8\}$$

Other more complex operations can be done including the _____, if the set is for example defined by a property rather than a finite or assumed infinite enumeration of elements.

a. Abelian P-root group
b. AKS primality test
c. ADE classification
d. Union

29. A _____ is a set G closed under a binary operation · satisfying the following 3 axioms:

- Associativity: For all a, b and c in G, (a · b) · c = a · (b · c.)
- Identity element: There exists an e∈G such that for all a in G, e · a = a · e = a.
- Inverse element: For each a in G, there is an element b in G such that a · b = b · a = e, where e is an identity element.

Basic examples for groups are the integers Z with addition operation, or rational numbers without zero Q{0} with multiplication. More generally, for any ring R, the units in R form a multiplicative _____ Groups include, however, much more general structures than the above.

a. Nilpotent group
b. Product of group subsets
c. Grigorchuk group
d. Group

30. In mathematics, group objects are certain generalizations of groups which are built on more complicated structures than sets. A typical example of a _____ is a topological group, a group whose underlying set is a topological space such that the group operations are continuous.

a. Bicommutant
b. Group object
c. Latin square property
d. P-groups

31. In mathematics, the _____ of homological algebra are derived functors of Hom functors. They were first used in algebraic topology, but are common in many areas of mathematics.

Let R be a ring and let Mod$_R$ be the category of modules over R. Let B be in Mod$_R$ and set

$$T(B) = \mathrm{Hom}_{\mathrm{Mod}_R}(A, B)$$, for fixed A in Mod$_R$.

a. ADE classification
b. Abelian P-root group
c. Ext functors
d. AKS primality test

32. The _____ and descending chain condition (DCC) are finiteness properties satisfied by certain algebraic structures, most importantly, ideals in a commutative ring. These conditions played an important role in the development of the structure theory of commutative rings in the works of David Hilbert, Emmy Noether, and Emil Artin. The conditions themselves can be stated in an abstract form, so that they make sense for any partially ordered set.

a. Ascending chain condition
b. Integral
c. Atomic domain
d. Invariant polynomial

33. In algebraic topology, a simplicial k-_____ is a formal linear combination of k-simplices.

Chapter 7. Modules and Categories

Integration is defined on chains by taking the linear combination of integrals over the simplices in the _____ with coefficients typically integers. The set of all k-chains forms a group and the sequence of these groups is called a _____ complex.

- a. Tesseract
- b. Bockstein homomorphism
- c. Chain
- d. Combinatorial topology

34. In linear algebra, a _____ is a set of vectors that, in a linear combination, can represent every vector in a given vector space or free module, and such that no element of the set can be represented as a linear combination of the others. In other words, a _____ is a linearly independent spanning set.
- a. Supergroup
- b. Minor
- c. Chirality
- d. Basis

35. In mathematics, a _____ is a free object in the category of modules. Given a set S, a _____ on S is a (particular construction of a) _____ with basis S.

Every vector space is free, and the free vector space on a set is a special case of a _____ on a set.

- a. Free module
- b. Simple modules
- c. Morita equivalence
- d. Relative tensor product

36. In mathematics, particularly in abstract algebra and homological algebra, the concept of _____ over a ring R is a more flexible generalisation of the idea of a free module (that is, a module with basis vectors.) Various equivalent characterizations of these modules are available.

Projective modules were first introduced in 1956 in the influential book Homological Algebra by Henri Cartan and Samuel Eilenberg.

- a. Projective module
- b. Hodge structure
- c. Homological algebra
- d. Tor functors

37. In category theory an _____ is a morphism f : X → Y which is right-cancellative in the sense that, for all morphisms $g_1, g_2 : Y \to Z$,

$$g_1 \circ f = g_2 \circ f \Rightarrow g_1 = g_2.$$

Epimorphisms are analogues of surjective functions, but they are not exactly the same. The dual of an _____ is a monomorphism (i.e. an _____ in a category C is a monomorphism in the dual category C^{op}.)

Many authors in abstract algebra and universal algebra define an _____ simply as an onto or surjective homomorphism.

a. Endomorphism
b. Isomorphism
c. ADE classification
d. Epimorphism

38. In mathematics, especially in the area of abstract algebra known as module theory, an _____ is a module Q that shares certain desirable properties with the Z-module Q of all rational numbers. Specifically, if Q is a submodule of some other module, then it is already a direct summand of that module; also, given a submodule of a module Y, then any module homomorphism from this submodule to Q can be extended to a homomorphism from all of Y to Q. This concept is dual to that of projective modules.

a. Abelian P-root group
b. ADE classification
c. AKS primality test
d. Injective module

39. In mathematics, the _____ construction in abstract algebra constructs an abelian group from a commutative monoid in the best possible way. It takes its name from the more general construction in category theory, introduced by Alexander Grothendieck in his fundamental work of the mid-1950s that resulted in the development of K-theory. The _____ is denoted by K or K_0.

a. Restriction of scalars
b. Grothendieck group
c. Coimage
d. Power set

40. In group theory, a branch of mathematics, the term _____ is used in two closely related senses:

- the _____ of a group is its cardinality, i.e. the number of its elements;
- the _____, sometimes period, of an element a of a group is the smallest positive integer m such that a^m = e (where e denotes the identity element of the group, and a^m denotes the product of m copies of a.) If no such m exists, we say that a has infinite _____. All elements of finite groups have finite _____.

We denote the _____ of a group G by ord(G) or $|G|$ and the _____ of an element a by ord(a) or $|a|$.

Example. The symmetric group S_3 has the following multiplication table.

This group has six elements, so ord(S_3) = 6.

a. Index calculus algorithm
b. Outer automorphism group
c. Order
d. Artin group

41. In mathematics, the _____ is a construction which allows one to 'glue together' several related objects, the precise manner of the gluing process being specified by morphisms between the objects. Inverse limits can be defined in any category.

a. AKS primality test
b. Abelian P-root group
c. ADE classification
d. Inverse limit

42. In mathematics, a _____ is a sequence whose elements become arbitrarily close to each other as the sequence progresses. To be more precise, by dropping enough (but still only a finite number of) terms from the start of the sequence, it is possible to make the maximum of the distances from any of the remaining elements to any other such element smaller than any preassigned, necessarily positive, value.

Chapter 7. Modules and Categories 83

In other words, suppose a pre-assigned positive real value ε is chosen.

- a. -module
- b. Cauchy sequence
- c. Distance matrix
- d. -equivalence

43. In commutative algebra, the term _____ refers to several related functors on topological rings and modules. _____ is similar to localization, and together they are among the most basic tools in analysing commutative rings. Complete commutative rings have simpler structure than the general ones, in large part, due to Hensel's lemma.
- a. Localization of a category
- b. Completion
- c. Localized
- d. Local analysis

44. In mathematics, the _____ systems were first described by Kurt Hensel in 1897. For each prime number p, the _____ system extends the ordinary arithmetic of the rational numbers in a way different from the extension of the rational number system to the real and complex number systems. The main use of these other systems is in number theory.
- a. Field extension
- b. Superreal numbers
- c. Local field
- d. P-adic number

45. In mathematics, a _____ is a colimit of a 'directed family of objects'. We will first give the definition for algebraic structures like groups and modules, and then the general definition which can be used in any category.
- a. -module
- b. Direct limit
- c. -equivalence
- d. 2-bridge knot

46. In mathematics, _____ are devices that make it possible to employ much of the analytical machinery of power series in settings that do not have natural notions of convergence. They are also useful, especially in combinatorics, for providing compact representations of sequences and multisets, and for finding closed formulas for recursively defined sequences; this is known as the method of generating functions.

A _____ can be loosely thought of as a polynomial with infinitely many terms.

- a. Matrix
- b. Multiplicative group
- c. Cokernel
- d. Formal power series

47. In the context of a module M over a ring R, the _____ of M is the largest semisimple quotient module of M if it exists.

For finite-dimensional k-algebras (k a field), if rad(M) denotes the intersection of all proper maximal submodules of M (the radical of the module), then the _____ of M is M/rad(M.) In the case of local rings with maximal ideal P, the _____ of M is M/PM.

- a. Puiseux series
- b. Krull dimension
- c. Top
- d. Local parameter

Chapter 8. Algebras

1. An _____ is a group satisfying the requirement that the result of applying the group operation to two group elements does not depend on their order Abelian groups generalize the arithmetic of addition of integers; they are named after Niels Henrik Abel.

The concept of an _____ is one of the first concepts encountered in undergraduate abstract algebra, with many other basic objects, such as a module and a vector space, being its refinements.

- a. ADE classification
- b. Algebraically compact
- c. Elementary abelian group
- d. Abelian group

2. In mathematics, an _____ is a morphism (or homomorphism) from a mathematical object to itself. For example, an _____ of a vector space V is a linear map $f: V \to V$, and an _____ of a group G is a group homomorphism $f: G \to G$. In general, we can talk about endomorphisms in any category.
- a. Isomorphism
- b. ADE classification
- c. Epimorphism
- d. Endomorphism

3. In abstract algebra, one associates to certain objects a ring, the object's _____, which encodes several internal properties of the object.
- a. Azumaya algebra
- b. Unipotent
- c. Irreducible ideal
- d. Endomorphism ring

4. A _____ is a set G closed under a binary operation · satisfying the following 3 axioms:

- Associativity: For all a, b and c in G, (a · b) · c = a · (b · c.)
- Identity element: There exists an e∈G such that for all a in G, e · a = a · e = a.
- Inverse element: For each a in G, there is an element b in G such that a · b = b · a = e, where e is an identity element.

Basic examples for groups are the integers Z with addition operation, or rational numbers without zero Q{0} with multiplication. More generally, for any ring R, the units in R form a multiplicative _____ Groups include, however, much more general structures than the above.

- a. Group
- b. Nilpotent group
- c. Product of group subsets
- d. Grigorchuk group

5. In mathematics, the _____ is any of various constructions to assign to a locally compact group an operator algebra (or more generally a Banach algebra), such that representations of the algebra are related to representations of the group. As such, they are similar to the group ring associated to a discrete group.

For the purposes of functional analysis, and in particular of harmonic analysis, one wishes to carry over the group ring construction to topological groups G. In case G is a locally compact Hausdorff group, G carries an essentially unique left-invariant countably additive Borel measure μ called Haar measure.

- a. CEP subgroup
- b. Homomorphism
- c. Spacetime algebra
- d. Group algebra

6. In mathematics, a _____ is a type of algebraic structure. There is some variation among mathematicians as to exactly what properties a _____ is required to have, as described in detail below. However, commonly a _____ is defined as a set together with two binary operations (usually called addition and multiplication), where each operation combines two elements to form a third element.
   a. -equivalence
   b. -module
   c. 2-bridge knot
   d. Ring

7. In mathematics, a polynomial P(X) is _____ over a field K if all of its irreducible factors have distinct roots in an algebraic closure of K - that is each irreducible factor of P(X) has distinct linear factors in some large enough field extension. There is, however, another, non-equivalent definition of separability. It says that P is _____ if and only if it is coprime to its formal derivative P'.
   a. Separable
   b. Field of fractions
   c. Global field
   d. Transcendence degree

8. In linear algebra, a _____ is a set of vectors that, in a linear combination, can represent every vector in a given vector space or free module, and such that no element of the set can be represented as a linear combination of the others. In other words, a _____ is a linearly independent spanning set.
   a. Supergroup
   b. Chirality
   c. Minor
   d. Basis

9. In mathematics, especially in elementary arithmetic, _____ is an arithmetic operation which is the inverse of multiplication.

Specifically, if c times b equals a, written:

$$c \times b = a$$

where b is not zero, then a divided by b equals c, written:

$$\frac{a}{b} = c$$

For instance,

$$\frac{6}{3} = 2$$

since

$$2 \times 3 = 6.$$

In the above expression, a is called the dividend, b the divisor and c the quotient.

a. -module
b. -equivalence
c. 2-bridge knot
d. Division

10. In abstract algebra, a _____ is a ring in which division is possible. More formally, a ring with 0 ≠ 1 is a _____ if every non-zero element a has a multiplicative inverse Division rings differ from fields only in that their multiplication is not required to be commutative.
a. Division ring
b. Square-free
c. Local ring
d. Ring homomorphism

11. In mathematics, especially in the area of abstract algebra known as ring theory, a _____ is a ring with 0 ≠ 1 such that ab = 0 implies that either a = 0 or b = 0 (the zero-product property.) That is, it is a nontrivial ring without left or right zero divisors. A commutative _____ is called an integral _____.
a. Coherent ring
b. Partially-ordered ring
c. Subring
d. Domain

12. In mathematics, _____ or factoring is the decomposition of an object ' href='/wiki/Matrix_(mathematics)'>matrix) into a product of other objects, or factors, which when multiplied together give the original. For example, the number 15 factors into primes as 3 × 5, and the polynomial $x^2 - 4$ factors as (x − 2)(x + 2.) In all cases, a product of simpler objects is obtained.
a. -module
b. -equivalence
c. 2-bridge knot
d. Factorization

13. In abstract algebra, a _____ is an algebraic structure with notions of addition, subtraction, multiplication and division, satisfying certain axioms. The most commonly used fields are the _____ of real numbers, the _____ of complex numbers, and the _____ of rational numbers, but there are also finite fields, fields of functions, various algebraic number fields, p-adic fields, and so forth.

Any _____ may be used as the scalars for a vector space, which is the standard general context for linear algebra.

a. Field
b. Tensor product of fields
c. Separable
d. Generic polynomial

14. _____, in mathematics, are a non-commutative number system that extends the complex numbers. The _____ were first described by Irish mathematician Sir William Rowan Hamilton in 1843 and applied to mechanics in three-dimensional space. They find uses in both theoretical and applied mathematics, in particular for calculations involving three-dimensional rotations , such as in 3D computer graphics, although they have been superseded in many applications by vectors and matrices.
a. Split-quaternions
b. Split-biquaternion
c. Generalized quaternion interpolation
d. Quaternions

15. In mathematics, a _____ is, roughly speaking, a commutative ring in which every element, with special exceptions, can be uniquely written as a product of prime elements, analogous to the fundamental theorem of arithmetic for the integers. Unique factorization domains are sometimes called factorial rings, following the terminology of Bourbaki.

Chapter 8. Algebras

Note that unique factorization domains appear in the following chain of class inclusions:

- Commutative rings ⊋ integral domains ⊋ unique factorization domains ⊋ principal ideal domains ⊋ Euclidean domains ⊋ fields

a. Absorption law
c. Unit ring
b. Unique factorization domain
d. Isomorphism class

16. In mathematics, a _____ is an algebraic structure whose main use is in studying geometric objects such as Lie groups and differentiable manifolds. Lie algebras were introduced to study the concept of infinitesimal transformations. The term '_____') was introduced by Hermann Weyl in the 1930s.
    a. Lie algebra
    c. Maximal torus
    b. Lorentz group
    d. Weyl group

17. In mathematics, a _____ is a subset of a ring, which contains the multiplicative identity and is itself a ring under the same binary operations. Naturally, those authors who do not require rings to contain a multiplicative identity do not require subrings to possess the identity (if it exists.) This leads to the added advantage that ideals become subrings
    a. Subring
    c. Poisson ring
    b. Semiperfect ring
    d. Kurosh problem

18. A _____ between two algebras over a field K, A and B, is a map $F : A \to B$ such that for all k in K and x,y in A,

- F(kx) = kF(x)

- F(x + y) = F(x) + F(y)

- F(xy) = F(x)F(y)

If F is bijective then F is said to be an isomorphism between A and B.

Let A = K[x] be the set of all polynomials over a field K and B be the set of all polynomial functions over K. Both A and B are algebras over K given by the standard multiplication and addition of polynomials and functions, respectively. We can map each f in A to $\hat{f}$ in B by the rule $\hat{f}(t) = f(t)$. A routine check shows that the mapping $f \mapsto \hat{f}$ is a _____ of the algebras A and B. If K is a finite field then let

$$p(x) = \Pi_{t \in K}(x - t).$$

p is a nonzero polynomial in K[x], however $p(t) = 0$ for all t in K, so $\hat{p} = 0$ is the zero function and the algebras are not isomorphic.

Chapter 8. Algebras

a. Tensor product of algebras
b. Frobenius matrix
c. Tensor algebra
d. Homomorphism

19. In ring theory or abstract algebra, a _____ is a function between two rings which respects the operations of addition and multiplication.

More precisely, if R and S are rings, then a _____ is a function f : R → S such that

- f(a + b) = f(a) + f(b) for all a and b in R
- f(ab) = f(a) f(b) for all a and b in R
- f(1) = 1

Naturally, if one does not require rings to have a multiplicative identity then the last condition is dropped.

The composition of two ring homomorphisms is a _____. It follows that the class of all rings forms a category with ring homomorphisms as the morphisms (cf.

a. Global dimension
b. Group ring
c. Krull ring
d. Ring homomorphism

20. In abstract algebra, the concept of a _____ over a ring is a generalization of the notion of vector space, where instead of requiring the scalars to lie in a field, the 'scalars' may lie in an arbitrary ring. Modules also generalize the notion of abelian groups, which are modules over $\mathbb{Z}$.

Thus, a _____, like a vector space, is an additive abelian group; a product is defined between elements of the ring and elements of the _____, and this multiplication is associative (when used with the multiplication in the ring) and distributive.

a. Semigroupoid
b. Module
c. Near-field
d. Goodman-Nguyen-van Fraassen algebra

21. This article deals with the ring of complex numbers integral over Z. For the general notion of _____, see Integrality.

In number theory, an _____ is a complex number that is a root of some monic polynomial (leading coefficient 1) with coefficients in Z. The set of all algebraic integers is closed under addition and multiplication and therefore is a subring of complex numbers denoted by A. The ring A is the integral closure of regular integers Z in complex numbers.

The ring of integers of a number field K, denoted by O_K, is the intersection of K and A: it can also be characterised as the maximal order of the field K. Each _____ belongs to the ring of integers of some number field.

a. Additive polynomial
c. Algebraic number theory
b. Adele ring
d. Algebraic integer

22. In mathematics, the _____ of a ring R, often denoted char(R), is defined to be the smallest number of times one must add the ring's multiplicative identity element (1) to itself to get the additive identity element (0); the ring is said to have _____ zero if this repeated sum never reaches the additive identity. That is, char(R) is the smallest positive number n such that

$$\underbrace{1 + \cdots + 1}_{n \text{ summands}} = 0$$

if such a number n exists, and 0 otherwise. The _____ may also be taken to be the exponent of the ring's additive group, that is, the smallest positive n such that

$$\underbrace{a + \cdots + a}_{n \text{ summands}} = 0$$

for every element a of the ring (again, if n exists; otherwise zero.)

a. Hereditary
c. Free ideal ring
b. Coherent ring
d. Characteristic

23. The _____ are natural numbers including 0 ' href='/wiki/0_(number)'>0, 1, 2, 3, ...) and their negatives (0, −1, −2, −3, ...). They are numbers that can be written without a fractional or decimal component, and fall within the set {...
a. Abelian P-root group
c. ADE classification
b. AKS primality test
d. Integers

24. In mathematics, a _____ in field theory is a special kind of basis for Galois extensions of finite degree, characterised as forming a single orbit for the Galois group. The _____ theorem states that any Galois extension of fields has a _____. In algebraic number theory the study of the more refined question of the existence of a normal integral basis is part of Galois module theory.
a. Symplectic vector space
c. Nonlinear eigenproblem
b. Spread of a matrix
d. Normal basis

25. In mathematics, the _____ of a number n is the number that, when added to n, yields zero. The _____ of F is denoted −F.

For example, the _____ of 7 is −7, because 7 + (−7) = 0, and the _____ of −0.3 is 0.3, because −0.3 + 0.3 = 0.

a. Interior algebra
c. Isomorphism class
b. Artinian ideal
d. Additive inverse

Chapter 8. Algebras

26. The term _____ is useful for describing certain algebraic structures. The term comes from the concept of an _____ binary operation which is a binary operation that draws from some _____ set. To be more specific, a left _____ binary operation on S over R is a function $f : R \times S \to S$ and a right _____ binary operation on S over R is a function $f : S \times R \to S$ where S is the set the operation is defined on, and R is the _____ set (the set the operation is defined over.)
   a. External
   b. Orthogonal
   c. Algebraic structure
   d. Unit ring

27. In mathematics, a _____ in one variable over a ring R is a linear combination of positive and negative powers of the variable with coefficients in R. Laurent polynomials in X form a ring denoted R[X, X⁻¹]. They differ from ordinary polynomials in that they may have terms of negative degree. The construction of Laurent polynomials may be iterated, leading to the ring of Laurent polynomials in several variables.
   a. Commutative ring
   b. Principal ideal ring
   c. Discrete valuation
   d. Laurent polynomial

28. In mathematics and, in particular, functional analysis, _____ is a mathematical operation on two functions f and g, producing a third function that is typically viewed as a modified version of one of the original functions. _____ is similar to cross-correlation. It has applications that include statistics, computer vision, image and signal processing, electrical engineering, and differential equations.
   a. -equivalence
   b. Convolution
   c. 2-bridge knot
   d. -module

29. In mathematics, the adjective _____ means that an object cannot be expressed as a product of more than one non-trivial factors in a given set. See also factorization.

For any field F, the ring of polynomials with coefficients in F is denoted by F[x].

   a. Integer-valued polynomial
   b. Alternating polynomial
   c. Irreducible
   d. Ehrhart polynomial

30. In abstract algebra, the _____ of a module is a measure of the module's 'size'. It is defined as the _____ of the longest ascending chain of submodules and is a generalization of the concept of dimension for vector spaces. The modules with finite _____ share many important properties with finite-dimensional vector spaces.
   a. Finitely generated module
   b. Length
   c. Supermodule
   d. Morita equivalence

31. In mathematics, the term _____ is used to describe an algebraic structures which in some sense cannot be divided by a smaller structure of the same type. Put another way, an algebraic structure is _____ if the kernel of every homomorphism is either the whole structure or a single element. Some examples are:

   - A group is called a _____ group if it does not contain a non-trivial proper normal subgroup.
   - A ring is called a _____ ring if it does not contain a non-trivial two sided ideal.
   - A module is called a _____ module if does not contain a non-trivial submodule.
   - An algebra is called a _____ algebra if does not contain a non-trivial two sided ideal.

The general pattern is that the structure admits no non-trivial congruence relations.

Chapter 8. Algebras

a. Commutativity
b. Simple
c. Linear combinations
d. Polarization identity

32. In mathematics, the _____ construction in abstract algebra constructs an abelian group from a commutative monoid in the best possible way. It takes its name from the more general construction in category theory, introduced by Alexander Grothendieck in his fundamental work of the mid-1950s that resulted in the development of K-theory. The _____ is denoted by K or K_0.

a. Coimage
b. Power set
c. Grothendieck group
d. Restriction of scalars

33. In abstract algebra, an _____ is a ring that satisfies the descending chain condition on ideals. They are also called Artin rings.

There are two classes of rings that have very similar properties:

- Rings whose underlying sets are finite.
- Rings that are finite-dimensional vector spaces over fields.

Emil Artin first discovered that the descending chain condition for ideals generalizes both classes of rings simultaneously. Artinian rings are named after him.

a. Unit
b. Artinian ring
c. Endomorphism ring
d. Irreducible ideal

34. In algebraic topology, a simplicial k-_____ is a formal linear combination of k-simplices.

Integration is defined on chains by taking the linear combination of integrals over the simplices in the _____ with coefficients typically integers. The set of all k-chains forms a group and the sequence of these groups is called a _____ complex.

a. Combinatorial topology
b. Bockstein homomorphism
c. Tesseract
d. Chain

35. In ring theory, a branch of abstract algebra, an _____ is a special subset of a ring. The _____ concept generalizes in an appropriate way some important properties of integers like 'even number' or 'multiple of 3'.

For instance, in rings one studies prime ideals instead of prime numbers, one defines coprime ideals as a generalization of coprime numbers, and one can prove a generalized Chinese remainder theorem about ideals.

a. Augmentation ideal
b. ADE classification
c. AKS primality test
d. Ideal

36. In ring theory, a branch of abstract algebra, the _____ of a ring R is an ideal of R which contains those elements of R which in a sense are 'close to zero'.

The _____ is denoted by J(R) and can be defined in the following equivalent ways:

- the intersection of all maximal left ideals.
- the intersection of all maximal right ideals.
- the intersection of all annihilators of simple left R-modules
- the intersection of all annihilators of simple right R-modules
- the intersection of all left primitive ideals.
- the intersection of all right primitive ideals.
- { x ∈ R : for every r ∈ R there exists u ∈ R with u (1-rx) = 1 }
- { x ∈ R : for every r ∈ R there exists u ∈ R with (1-xr) u = 1 }
- if R is commutative, the intersection of all maximal ideals in R.
- the largest ideal I such that for all x ∈ I, 1-x is invertible in R

Note that the last property does not mean that every element x of R such that 1-x is invertible must be an element of J(R.) Also, if R is not commutative, then J(R) is not necessarily equal to the intersection of all two-sided maximal ideals in R.

A _____ may also be defined for rings without an identity (or unity) element.

a. Jacobson radical
b. Radical of an ring
c. Primitive ideal
d. Principal ideal

37. The _____ of a Lie algebra $\mathfrak{g}$ is a particular ideal of $\mathfrak{g}$.

Let $\mathfrak{g}$ be a Lie algebra. The _____ of $\mathfrak{g}$ is defined as the largest solvable ideal of $\mathfrak{g}$.

a. Class sum
b. Cyclically reduced word
c. Garside element
d. Radical

38. In mathematics, a Lie algebra is _____ if it is a direct sum of simple Lie algebras, i.e., non-abelian Lie algebras $\mathfrak{g}$ whose only ideals are {0} and $\mathfrak{g}$ itself. It is called reductive if it is the sum of a _____ and an abelian Lie algebra.

Let $\mathfrak{g}$ be a finite-dimensional Lie algebra over a field of characteristic 0.

a. Dixmier conjecture
b. Tensor product of algebras
c. Graded algebra
d. Semisimple

39. In mathematics, specifically module theory, annihilators are a concept that generalizes torsion and orthogonal complement.

Let R be a ring, and let M be a left R-module. Choose a subset S of M. The _____, Ann$_R$S, of S is the set of all elements r in R such that for each s in S, rs = 0: it is the set of all elements that annihilate S (the elements for which S is torsion.)

a. Annihilator
b. Augmentation ideal
c. AKS primality test
d. ADE classification

40. In abstract algebra, the _____ is the ring of differential operators with polynomial coefficients (in one variable),

$$f_n(X)\partial_X^n + \cdots + f_1(X)\partial_X + f_0(X).$$

More precisely, let F be a field, and let F[X] be the ring of polynomials in one variable, X, with coefficients in F. Then each f_i lies in F[X]. ∂_X is the derivative with respect to X. The algebra is generated by X and ∂_X.

The _____ is an example of a simple ring that is not a matrix ring over a division ring.

a. Normed division algebra
b. Poisson algebra
c. Hereditary C*-subalgebra
d. Weyl algebra

41. In mathematics, in the field of group theory, a _____ of a finite group is a quasisimple subnormal subgroup. Any two distinct components commute. The product of all the components is the layer of the group.

a. Component
b. Wreath product
c. Stallings' theorem about ends of groups
d. Group homomorphism

42. Let G be a finite group with conjugacy class C. Then the _____

$$\overline{C} = \sum_{c \in C} c$$

is an element of the center of the group algebra $Z(\mathbb{C}G)$.

a. Bifundamental representation
b. Harmonic polynomial
c. Class sum
d. Bimonster

43. In ring theory, a left _____ is a ring which has a faithful simple left module. Examples include matrix algebras over division rings, non-commutative polynomial rings and simple Artinian rings.

A ring R is said to be a left _____ if and only if it has a faithful simple left R-module.

a. Flat map
b. Brauer group
c. Primitive ring
d. Multivector

Chapter 8. Algebras

44. In mathematics, an _____ is an ideal in any group ring. If G is a group and R a commutative ring, there is a ring homomorphism ε, called the augmentation map, from the group ring

R[G]

to R, defined by taking a sum

$$\sum r_i g_i$$

to

$$\sum r_i.$$

Here r_i is an element of R and g_i an element of G. The sums are finite, by definition of the group ring. In less formal terms,

$$\varepsilon(g)$$

is defined as 1_R whatever the element g in G, and ε is then extended to a homomorphism of R-modules in the obvious way.

a. Augmentation ideal
c. Ideal
b. ADE classification
d. AKS primality test

45. In algebraic geometry, divisors are a generalization of codimension one subvarieties of algebraic varieties; two different generalizations are in common use, Cartier divisors and Weil divisors The concepts agree on non-singular varieties over algebraically closed fields.

A Weil _____ is a locally finite linear combination (with integral coefficients) of irreducible subvarieties of codimension one.

a. Picard group
c. Divisor
b. Linear system of divisors
d. Lefschetz pencil

46. In abstract algebra, a nonzero element a of a ring is a left _____ if there exists a nonzero b such that ab = 0. Right zero divisors are defined analogously, that is, a nonzero element a of a ring is a right _____ if there exists a nonzero c such that ca = 0. An element that is both a left and a right _____ is simply called a _____.

a. Polynomial expression
c. BCK algebras
b. Matrix
d. Zero divisor

47. The concept of _____ treated here occurs in mathematics.

Let R be a commutative ring with unity, and let M, N and L be three R-modules.

Chapter 8. Algebras

A _____ is any R-bilinear map $e : M \times N \to L$.

   a. Delta operator
   c. Conjugate transpose
   b. Pairing
   d. Projection-valued measure

48. In mathematics, the _____, denoted by ⊗, may be applied in different contexts to vectors, matrices, tensors, vector spaces, algebras, topological vector spaces, and modules. In each case the significance of the symbol is the same: the most general bilinear operation. In some contexts, this product is also referred to as outer product.
   a. Near-semiring
   c. Cycle graph
   b. Linear span
   d. Tensor product

49. In abstract algebra a _____ is an abelian group that is both a left and a right module, such that the left and right multiplications are compatible. Besides appearing naturally in many parts of mathematics, bimodules play a clarifying role, in the sense that many of the relationships between left and right modules become simpler when they are expressed in terms of bimodules.

If R and S are two rings, then an R-S-_____ is an abelian group M such that:

1. M is a left R-module and a right S-module.
2. For all r in R, s in S and m in M:

      (rm)s = r(ms.)

An R-R-_____ is also known as an R-_____.

   a. Socle
   c. Semisimple module
   b. Fitting lemma
   d. Bimodule

50. In geometry, a _____ is a subset of n-dimensional space that is congruent to a Euclidean space of lower dimension. The flats in two-dimensional space are points and lines, and the flats in three-dimensional space are points, lines, and planes. In n-dimensional space, there are flats of every dimension from 0 to n - 1.
   a. -module
   c. Similarity
   b. -equivalence
   d. Flat

51. In abstract algebra, a _____ over a ring R is an R-module M such that taking the tensor product over R with M preserves exact sequences. A module is faithfully flat if taking the tensor product with a sequence produces an exact sequence if and only if the original sequence is exact.

Vector spaces over a field are flat modules.

   a. Resolution
   c. Hodge structure
   b. Koszul-Tate resolution
   d. Flat module

52. The _____ and descending chain condition (DCC) are finiteness properties satisfied by certain algebraic structures, most importantly, ideals in a commutative ring. These conditions played an important role in the development of the structure theory of commutative rings in the works of David Hilbert, Emmy Noether, and Emil Artin. The conditions themselves can be stated in an abstract form, so that they make sense for any partially ordered set.
  a. Atomic domain
  b. Integral
  c. Ascending chain condition
  d. Invariant polynomial

53. In abstract algebra, an _____ is a bijective map f such that both f and its inverse f^{-1} are homomorphisms, i.e., structure-preserving mappings. In the more general setting of category theory, an _____ is a morphism f:X→Y in a category for which there exists an 'inverse' f^{-1}:Y→X, with the property that both $f^{-1}f=id_X$ and $ff^{-1}=id_Y$.

Informally, an _____ is a kind of mapping between objects, which shows a relationship between two properties or operations.

  a. Isomorphism
  b. Endomorphism
  c. ADE classification
  d. Epimorphism

54. In mathematics, a _____ is (most commonly) a special kind of function from a group to a field (such as the complex numbers.) There are at least two distinct, but overlapping meanings. Other uses of the word '_____' are almost always qualified.
  a. Trivial representation
  b. Deligne-Lusztig theory
  c. Real representation
  d. Character

55. In abstract algebra, _____ is a relationship defined between rings that preserves many ring-theoretic properties. It is named after Japanese mathematician Kiiti Morita who defined equivalence and a similar notion of duality in 1958.

Rings are commonly studied in terms of their modules, as modules can be viewed as representations of rings.

  a. Stably free module
  b. Tensor product of modules
  c. Free module
  d. Morita equivalence

56. In mathematics, the _____, denoted by ⊗, is an operation on two matrices of arbitrary size resulting in a block matrix. It is a special case of a tensor product. The _____ should not be confused with the usual matrix multiplication, which is an entirely different operation.
  a. Schur decomposition
  b. Totally positive matrix
  c. Laplace expansion
  d. Kronecker product

57. A _____ is a symbol that stands for a value that may vary; the term usually occurs in opposition to constant, which is a symbol for a non-varying value, i.e. completely fixed or fixed in the context of use. The concepts of constants and variables are fundamental to all modern mathematics, science, engineering, and computer programming.

Much of the basic theory for which we use variables today, such as school geometry and algebra, was developed thousands of years ago, but the use of symbolic formulae and variables is only several hundreds of years old.

a. 2-bridge knot
c. -equivalence

b. -module
d. Variable

58. In mathematics, there are several meanings of _____ depending on the subject.

A _____, usually denoted by ° (the _____ symbol), is a measurement of plane angle, representing $\frac{1}{360}$ of a full rotation. When that angle is with respect to a reference meridian, it indicates a location along a great circle of a sphere, such as Earth , Mars, or the celestial sphere.

a. Median algebra
c. Degree

b. Relation algebra
d. Symmetric difference

59. In mathematics, a _____ is a rectangular array of numbers. This way, matrices can record data that depend on multiple parameters. In particular they are used to keep track of the coefficients of multiple linear equations. Matrices are closely connected to linear transformations, which are higher-dimensional analogs of linear functions, i.e., functions of the form f(x) = c Â· x, where c is a constant. This map corresponds to a _____ with one row and column, with entry c. In addition to a number of elementary, entrywise operations such as _____ addition a key notion is _____ multiplication, which displays a number of features not encountered in numbers; for example, products of matrices depend on the order of the factors, unlike products of real numbers, say, where c Â· d = d Â· c for any two numbers c and d.

a. Heap
c. Polynomial expression

b. Matrix
d. Commutativity

60. In several fields of mathematics the term _____ is used with different but closely related meanings. They all relate to the notion of mapping the elements of a set to other elements of the same set, i.e., exchanging (or 'permuting') elements of a set.

The general concept of _____ can be defined more formally in different contexts:

In combinatorics, a _____ is usually understood to be a sequence containing each element from a finite set once, and only once.

a. Binary function
c. Rupture field

b. Near-field
d. Permutation

61. In mathematics, in matrix theory, a _____ is a square (0,1)-matrix that has exactly one entry 1 in each row and each column and 0's elsewhere. Each such matrix represents a specific permutation of m elements and, when used to multiply another matrix, can produce that permutation in the rows or columns of the other matrix.

Given a permutation π of m elements,

$$\pi : \{1,\ldots,m\} \to \{1,\ldots,m\}$$

given in two-line form by

$$\begin{pmatrix} 1 & 2 & \cdots & m \\ \pi(1) & \pi(2) & \cdots & \pi(m) \end{pmatrix},$$

its _____ is the m × m matrix P_π whose entries are all 0 except that in row i, the entry π(i) equals 1.

a. Hessenberg matrix
b. Permutation matrix
c. Skew-symmetric
d. Main diagonal

62. In mathematics, and in particular the theory of group representations, the _____ of a group G is the linear representation afforded by the group action of G on itself.

To say that G acts on itself by multiplication is tautological. If we consider this action as a permutation representation it is characterised as having a single orbit and stabilizer the identity subgroup {e} of G. The _____ of G, for a given field K, is the linear representation made by taking the permutation representation as a set of basis vectors of a vector space over K. The significance is that while the permutation representation doesn't decompose - it is transitive - the _____ in general breaks up into smaller representations.

a. Monomial representation
b. Gelfand pair
c. Regular representation
d. Matrix coefficient

63. In mathematics, especially in the fields of group theory and representation theory of groups, a _____ is a function f on a group G, such that f is constant on the conjugacy classes of G. In other words, f is invariant under the conjugation map on G. Such functions play a basic role in representation theory.

The character of a linear representation of G over a field K is always a _____ with values in K. The class functions form the center of the group ring K[G]. Here a _____ f is identified with the element $\sum_{g \in G} f(g)g$.

a. Class function
b. Generalized polygon
c. Double coset
d. Group theory

64. In mathematics, two vectors are _____ if they are perpendicular, i.e., they form a right angle. The word comes from the Greek á½€ρθίŒς , meaning 'straight', and γωνῖα (gonia), meaning 'angle'. For example, a subway and the street above, although they do not physically intersect, are _____ if they cross at a right angle.
a. Embedding
b. Expression
c. Unital
d. Orthogonal

65. In the various branches of mathematics that fall under the heading of abstract algebra, the _____ of a homomorphism measures the degree to which the homomorphism fails to be injective. An important special case is the _____ of a matrix, also called the null space.

The definition of _____ takes various forms in various contexts.

a. Monomial basis
b. Completing the square
c. Kernel
d. K-theory

66. In mathematics, and in particular group representation theory, the _____ is one of the major general operations for passing from a representation of a subgroup H to a representation of the (whole) group G itself. It was initially defined as a construction by Frobenius, for linear representations of finite groups. It includes as special cases the action of G on the cosets G/H by permutation, which is the case of the _____ starting with the trivial one-dimensional representation of H. If H = {e} this becomes the regular representation of G. Therefore induced representations are rich objects, in the sense that they include or detect many interesting representations.

a. Order
b. Orbifold notation
c. Outer automorphism
d. Induced representation

67. In mathematics, the _____ of a finite group is an algebraic construction that encodes the different ways the group can act on finite sets. The ideas were introduced by William Burnside at the end of the nineteenth Century, but the algebraic ring structure is a more recent development, probably due to Andreas Dress (1969.)

Given a finite group G, the elements of its _____ $\Omega(G)$ are the formal differences of isomorphism classes of finite G-sets.

a. Perfect group
b. Burnside ring
c. Coset enumeration
d. Group

68. In ring theory, a branch of abstract algebra, a _____ is an ideal I in a ring R that is generated by a single element a of R.

More specifically:

- a left _____ of R is a subset of R of the form Ra := {ra : r in R};
- a right _____ is a subset of the form aR := {ar : r in R};
- a two-sided _____ is a subset of the form RaR := {$r_1 a s_1$ + ... + $r_n a s_n$: $r_1, s_1, ..., r_n, s_n$ in R}.

If R is a commutative ring, then the above three notions are all the same. In that case, it is common to write the ideal generated by a as (a.)

Not all ideals are principal.

a. Radical of an ring
b. Primitive ideal
c. Radical of an ideal
d. Principal ideal

69. In abstract algebra, a _____ i.e., can be generated by a single element. More generally, a principal ring is a nonzero commutative ring whose ideals are principal, although some authors (e.g., Bourbaki) refers to Principal ideal domains as principal rings. The distinction being that a principal ideal ring may have zero divisors whereas a _____ cannot.

a. Nilradical
b. Minimal prime
c. Discrete valuation
d. Principal ideal domain

70. In mathematics, a _____ is a transitive permutation group on a finite set, such that no non-trivial element fixes more than one point and some non-trivial element fixes a point. They are named after F. G. Frobenius.

The subgroup H of a _____ G fixing a point of the set X is called the Frobenius complement.

a. Permutation group
b. Symmetric group
c. Frobenius group
d. Parker vector

71. In discrete mathematics and predominantly in set theory, a _____ is a concept used in comparisons of sets to refer to the unique values of one set in relation to another. The terms 'absolute' and 'relative' _____ refer to more specific applications of the concept, with universal complements referring to elements unique to the universal set and the latter referring to the unique elements of one set in relation to another. In this image, the universal set is represented by the border of the image, and the set A as a disc.

a. Pointed set
b. -module
c. -equivalence
d. Complement

72. In mathematics, more specifically in abstract algebra, the _____, proved by Ferdinand Georg Frobenius in 1877, characterizes the finite dimensional associative division algebras over the real numbers. The theorem proves that the only associative division algebra which is not commutative over the real numbers is the quaternions.

If D is a finite dimensional division algebra over the real numbers R then one of the following cases holds

- D = R
- D = C (complex numbers)
- D = H (quaternions.)

The main ingredients for the following proof are the Cayley-Hamilton Theorem and the Fundamental theorem of algebra.

We can consider D as a finite-dimensional R-vector space.

a. Tensor algebra
b. Dixmier conjecture
c. Garside element
d. Frobenius theorem

Chapter 9. Advanced Linear Algebra

1. In group theory, a branch of mathematics, the term _____ is used in two closely related senses:

   - the _____ of a group is its cardinality, i.e. the number of its elements;
   - the _____, sometimes period, of an element a of a group is the smallest positive integer m such that a^m = e (where e denotes the identity element of the group, and a^m denotes the product of m copies of a.) If no such m exists, we say that a has infinite _____. All elements of finite groups have finite _____.

   We denote the _____ of a group G by ord(G) or |G| and the _____ of an element a by ord(a) or |a|.

   Example. The symmetric group S_3 has the following multiplication table.

   This group has six elements, so ord(S_3) = 6.

   a. Outer automorphism group
   b. Index calculus algorithm
   c. Artin group
   d. Order

2. In abstract algebra, the concept of a _____ over a ring is a generalization of the notion of vector space, where instead of requiring the scalars to lie in a field, the 'scalars' may lie in an arbitrary ring. Modules also generalize the notion of abelian groups, which are modules over $\mathbb{Z}$.

   Thus, a _____, like a vector space, is an additive abelian group; a product is defined between elements of the ring and elements of the _____, and this multiplication is associative (when used with the multiplication in the ring) and distributive.

   a. Semigroupoid
   b. Near-field
   c. Goodman-Nguyen-van Fraassen algebra
   d. Module

3. In abstract algebra, the term _____ refers to a number of concepts related to elements of finite order in groups and to the failure of modules to be free.

   Let G be a group. An element g of G is called a _____ element if g has finite order.

   a. Torsion subgroup
   b. Divisible group
   c. Torsion
   d. Cyclic group

4. In geometry, a _____ is a subset of n-dimensional space that is congruent to a Euclidean space of lower dimension. The flats in two-dimensional space are points and lines, and the flats in three-dimensional space are points, lines, and planes. In n-dimensional space, there are flats of every dimension from 0 to n - 1.
   a. Flat
   b. -equivalence
   c. -module
   d. Similarity

5. In mathematics, in the field of group theory, a _____ of a finite group is a quasisimple subnormal subgroup. Any two distinct components commute. The product of all the components is the layer of the group.

a. Component
c. Group homomorphism
b. Stallings' theorem about ends of groups
d. Wreath product

6. In mathematics, more specifically in abstract algebra, _____ provides a connection between field theory and group theory. Using _____, certain problems in field theory can be reduced to group theory, which is in some sense simpler and better understood.

Originally Galois used permutation groups to describe how the various roots of a given polynomial equation are related to each other.

a. Simple extension
c. Separable
b. Galois group
d. Galois theory

7. In mathematics, the _____ of a ring R, often denoted char(R), is defined to be the smallest number of times one must add the ring's multiplicative identity element (1) to itself to get the additive identity element (0); the ring is said to have _____ zero if this repeated sum never reaches the additive identity. That is, char(R) is the smallest positive number n such that

$$\underbrace{1 + \cdots + 1}_{n \text{ summands}} = 0$$

if such a number n exists, and 0 otherwise. The _____ may also be taken to be the exponent of the ring's additive group, that is, the smallest positive n such that

$$\underbrace{a + \cdots + a}_{n \text{ summands}} = 0$$

for every element a of the ring (again, if n exists; otherwise zero.)

a. Free ideal ring
c. Hereditary
b. Coherent ring
d. Characteristic

8. In algebraic geometry, divisors are a generalization of codimension one subvarieties of algebraic varieties; two different generalizations are in common use, Cartier divisors and Weil divisors The concepts agree on non-singular varieties over algebraically closed fields.

A Weil _____ is a locally finite linear combination (with integral coefficients) of irreducible subvarieties of codimension one.

a. Picard group
c. Divisor
b. Linear system of divisors
d. Lefschetz pencil

9. In algebra, the _____ of a module over a principal ideal domain occur in one form of the structure theorem for finitely generated modules over a principal ideal domain.

If R is a PID and M a finitely generated R-module, then M is isomorphic to a unique sum of the form

$$M \cong R^r \oplus \bigoplus_i R/(q_i)$$

where $q_i \neq 1$ and the (q_i) are primary ideals.

The ideals (q_i) are unique (up to order); the elements q_i are unique up to associatedness, and are called the _____.

a. Injective hull
c. Extension of scalars

b. Invariant factors
d. Elementary divisors

10. The _____ of a module over a principal ideal domain occur in one form of the structure theorem for finitely generated modules over a principal ideal domain.

If R is a PID and M a finitely generated R-module, then

$$M \cong R^r \oplus R/(a_1) \oplus R/(a_2) \oplus \cdots \oplus R/(a_m)$$

for some $r \in \mathbb{Z}_0^+$ and nonzero elements $a_1, \ldots, a_m \in R$ for which $a_1 \mid \cdots \mid a_m$. The nonnegative integer r is called the free rank or Betti number of the module M, while $a_1, \ldots, a_m$ are the _____ of M and are unique up to associatedness.

a. Extension of scalars
c. Injective hull

b. Invariant factors
d. Invariant basis number

11. An _____ is a group satisfying the requirement that the result of applying the group operation to two group elements does not depend on their order Abelian groups generalize the arithmetic of addition of integers; they are named after Niels Henrik Abel.

The concept of an _____ is one of the first concepts encountered in undergraduate abstract algebra, with many other basic objects, such as a module and a vector space, being its refinements.

a. Algebraically compact
c. Abelian group

b. Elementary abelian group
d. ADE classification

12. A _____ is a set G closed under a binary operation · satisfying the following 3 axioms:

- Associativity: For all a, b and c in G, (a · b) · c = a · (b · c.)
- Identity element: There exists an e∈G such that for all a in G, e · a = a · e = a.
- Inverse element: For each a in G, there is an element b in G such that a · b = b · a = e, where e is an identity element.

Basic examples for groups are the integers Z with addition operation, or rational numbers without zero Q{0} with multiplication. More generally, for any ring R, the units in R form a multiplicative _____ Groups include, however, much more general structures than the above.

a. Grigorchuk group
b. Nilpotent group
c. Product of group subsets
d. Group

13. In linear algebra, a _____ is a set of vectors that, in a linear combination, can represent every vector in a given vector space or free module, and such that no element of the set can be represented as a linear combination of the others. In other words, a _____ is a linearly independent spanning set.

a. Minor
b. Chirality
c. Basis
d. Supergroup

14. In mathematics, especially in the field of module theory, the concept of _____ provides a generalization of direct summand, a type of particularly well-behaved piece of a module. Pure modules are complementary to flat modules and generalize Prüfer's notion of pure subgroups. While flat modules are those modules which leave short exact sequences exact after tensoring, a _____ defines a short exact sequence that remains exact after tensoring with any module.

a. Simple modules
b. Finitely generated module
c. Pure submodule
d. Comodule

15. In linear algebra, the _____ of the monic polynomial

$$p(t) = c_0 + c_1 t + \ldots + c_{n-1} t^{n-1} + t^n$$

is the square matrix defined as

$$C(p) = \begin{bmatrix} 0 & 0 & \ldots & 0 & -c_0 \\ 1 & 0 & \ldots & 0 & -c_1 \\ 0 & 1 & \ldots & 0 & -c_2 \\ \vdots & \vdots & \vdots & \vdots & \vdots \\ 0 & 0 & \ldots & 1 & -c_{n-1} \end{bmatrix}.$$

With this convention, and writing the basis as $v_1, \ldots, v_n$, one has $Cv_i = C^{i-1} v_1 = v_{i+1}$ (for i < n), and v_1 generates V as a K[C]-module: C cycles basis vectors.

Some authors use the transpose of this matrix, which (dually) cycles coordinates, and is more convenient for some purposes, like linear recursive relations.

The characteristic polynomial as well as the minimal polynomial of C(p) are equal to p; in this sense, the matrix C(p) is the 'companion' of the polynomial p.

a. Levinson recursion
b. Matrix representation
c. Wilkinson matrices
d. Companion matrix

Chapter 9. Advanced Linear Algebra

16. In mathematics, especially in the area of abstract algebra known as ring theory, a _____ is a ring with 0 ≠ 1 such that ab = 0 implies that either a = 0 or b = 0 (the zero-product property.) That is, it is a nontrivial ring without left or right zero divisors. A commutative _____ is called an integral _____.
    a. Partially-ordered ring
    b. Coherent ring
    c. Subring
    d. Domain

17. In mathematics, _____ or factoring is the decomposition of an object ' href='/wiki/Matrix_(mathematics)'>matrix) into a product of other objects, or factors, which when multiplied together give the original. For example, the number 15 factors into primes as 3 × 5, and the polynomial $x^2 - 4$ factors as (x − 2)(x + 2.) In all cases, a product of simpler objects is obtained.
    a. 2-bridge knot
    b. Factorization
    c. -equivalence
    d. -module

18. In mathematics, a _____ is a rectangular array of numbers. This way, matrices can record data that depend on multiple parameters. In particular they are used to keep track of the coefficients of multiple linear equations. Matrices are closely connected to linear transformations, which are higher-dimensional analogs of linear functions, i.e., functions of the form f(x) = c · x, where c is a constant. This map corresponds to a _____ with one row and column, with entry c. In addition to a number of elementary, entrywise operations such as _____ addition a key notion is _____ multiplication, which displays a number of features not encountered in numbers; for example, products of matrices depend on the order of the factors, unlike products of real numbers, say, where c · d = d · c for any two numbers c and d.
    a. Polynomial expression
    b. Commutativity
    c. Heap
    d. Matrix

19. In mathematics, a _____ is, roughly speaking, a commutative ring in which every element, with special exceptions, can be uniquely written as a product of prime elements, analogous to the fundamental theorem of arithmetic for the integers. Unique factorization domains are sometimes called factorial rings, following the terminology of Bourbaki.

Note that unique factorization domains appear in the following chain of class inclusions:

- Commutative rings >⊃ integral domains >⊃ unique factorization domains >⊃ principal ideal domains >⊃ Euclidean domains >⊃ fields

    a. Unit ring
    b. Absorption law
    c. Isomorphism class
    d. Unique factorization domain

20. Generally, in mathematics, a _____ of an object is a standard way of presenting that object.

_____ can also mean a differential form that is defined in a natural (canonical) way; see below.

Suppose we have some set S of objects, with an equivalence relation.

    a. Brahmagupta's identity
    b. Cylindrical algebraic decomposition
    c. Monomial basis
    d. Canonical form

21. In linear algebra, the _____ states that every square matrix over the real or complex field satisfies its own characteristic equation.

More precisely; if A is the given n×n matrix and I_n is the n×n identity matrix, then the characteristic polynomial of A is defined as:

where 'det' is the determinant function. The _____ states that substituting the matrix A in the characteristic polynomial (which involves multiplying its constant term by I_n, since that is the zeroth power of A) results in the zero matrix:

The _____ also holds for square matrices over commutative rings.

a. -module
b. Cayley-Hamilton theorem
c. -equivalence
d. 2-bridge knot

22. In a totally ordered set all elements are mutually comparable, so such a set can have at most one minimal element and at most one maximal element. Then, due to mutual comparability, the minimal element will also be the least element and the maximal element will also be the greatest element. Thus in a totally ordered set we can simply use the terms _____ and maximum.

a. -equivalence
b. -module
c. 2-bridge knot
d. Minimum

23. A _____ or matrix polynomial is a matrix whose elements are univariate or multivariate polynomials.

A univariate _____ P of degree p is defined as:

$$P = \sum_{n=0}^{p} A(n)x^n = A(0) + A(1)x + A(2)x^2 + \cdots + A(p)x^p$$

where A(i) denotes a matrix of constant coefficients, and A(p) is non-zero. Thus a _____ is the matrix-equivalent of a polynomial, with each element of the matrix satisfying the definition of a polynomial of degree p.

a. Wilkinson matrices
b. Paley construction
c. Skew-symmetric
d. Polynomial matrix

24. In mathematics, a _____ is an algebraic structure whose main use is in studying geometric objects such as Lie groups and differentiable manifolds. Lie algebras were introduced to study the concept of infinitesimal transformations. The term '_____') was introduced by Hermann Weyl in the 1930s.

a. Maximal torus
b. Weyl group
c. Lorentz group
d. Lie algebra

Chapter 9. Advanced Linear Algebra

25. In mathematics, an element x of a ring R is called _____ if there exists some positive integer n such that $x^n = 0$.

The term was introduced by Benjamin Peirce in the context of elements of an algebra that vanish when raised to a power.

- This definition can be applied in particular to square matrices. The matrix

$$A = \begin{pmatrix} 0 & 1 & 0 \\ 0 & 0 & 1 \\ 0 & 0 & 0 \end{pmatrix}$$

is _____ because $A^3 = 0$. See _____ matrix for more.

a. Hochschild homology
b. Ring of integers
c. Nilpotent
d. Product ring

26. In linear algebra, _____ is an efficient algorithm for solving systems of linear equations, finding the rank of a matrix, and calculating the inverse of an invertible square matrix. _____ is named after German mathematician and scientist Carl Friedrich Gauss.

Elementary row operations are used to reduce a matrix to row echelon form.

a. 2-bridge knot
b. -module
c. -equivalence
d. Gaussian elimination

27. In mathematics, an _____ is a simple matrix which differs from the identity matrix in a minimal way. The elementary matrices generate the general linear group of invertible matrices, and left (respectively, right) multiplication by an _____ represent elementary row operations (respectively, elementary column operations.)

In algebraic K-theory, 'elementary matrices' refers only to the row-addition matrices.

a. Elementary matrix
b. Orientation
c. Orthogonalization
d. Orthonormal basis

28. The _____ is a normal form that can be defined for any matrix (not necessarily square) with entries in a principal ideal domain (PID.) The _____ of a matrix is diagonal, and can be obtained from the original matrix by multiplying on the left and right by invertible square matrices. In particular, the integers are a PID, so one can always calculate the _____ of an integer matrix.

a. Smith normal form
b. Nullity theorem
c. Matrix decomposition
d. Sparse graph code

29. In mathematics, an _____ is a vector space with the additional structure of inner product. This additional structure associates each pair of vectors in the space with a scalar quantity known as the inner product of the vectors. Inner products allow the rigorous introduction of intuitive geometrical notions such as the length of a vector or the angle between two vectors.

108 *Chapter 9. Advanced Linear Algebra*

    a. ADE classification
    b. Inner product space
    c. AKS primality test
    d. Abelian P-root group

30. The set of all symmetry operations considered, on all objects in a set X, can be modeled as a group action g : G × X → X, where the image of g in G and x in X is written as g·x. If, for some g, g·x = y then x and y are said to be symmetrical to each other. For each object x, operations g for which g·x = x form a group, the _____ of the object, a subgroup of G. If the _____ of x is the trivial group then x is said to be asymmetric, otherwise symmetric.
    a. -module
    b. -equivalence
    c. 2-bridge knot
    d. Symmetry group

31. In discrete mathematics and predominantly in set theory, a _____ is a concept used in comparisons of sets to refer to the unique values of one set in relation to another. The terms 'absolute' and 'relative' _____ refer to more specific applications of the concept, with universal complements referring to elements unique to the universal set and the latter referring to the unique elements of one set in relation to another. In this image, the universal set is represented by the border of the image, and the set A as a disc.
    a. -equivalence
    b. -module
    c. Pointed set
    d. Complement

32. In mathematics, two vectors are _____ if they are perpendicular, i.e., they form a right angle. The word comes from the Greek ἀνρθΐŒς , meaning 'straight', and γωνῖα (gonia), meaning 'angle'. For example, a subway and the street above, although they do not physically intersect, are _____ if they cross at a right angle.
    a. Expression
    b. Embedding
    c. Unital
    d. Orthogonal

33. In the mathematical fields of linear algebra and functional analysis, the _____ $W^\perp$ of a subspace W of an inner product space V is the set of all vectors in V that are orthogonal to every vector in W, i.e., it is

$$W^\perp = \{x \in V : \langle x, y \rangle = 0 \text{ for all } y \in W\}.$$

Informally, it is called the perp, short for perpendicular complement.

The _____ is always closed in the metric topology. In finite-dimensional spaces, that is merely an instance of the fact that all subspaces of a vector space are closed.

    a. Invariant subspace
    b. Euclidean subspace
    c. Orthogonal complement
    d. Independent equation

34. In mathematics, the linear algebra concept of _____ can be applied in the context of a finite extension L/K, by using the field trace. This requires the property that the field trace $Tr_{L/K}$ provides a non-degenerate quadratic form over K. This can be guaranteed if the extension is separable; it is automatically true if K is a perfect field, and hence in the cases where K is finite, or of characteristic zero.

A _____ isn't a concrete basis like the polynomial basis or the normal basis; rather it provides a way of using a second basis for computations.

a. Dual basis
b. Column space
c. Segre classification
d. Linear complementarity problem

35. In ring theory, a branch of abstract algebra, an _____ is a special subset of a ring. The _____ concept generalizes in an appropriate way some important properties of integers like 'even number' or 'multiple of 3'.

For instance, in rings one studies prime ideals instead of prime numbers, one defines coprime ideals as a generalization of coprime numbers, and one can prove a generalized Chinese remainder theorem about ideals.

a. ADE classification
b. AKS primality test
c. Augmentation ideal
d. Ideal

36. In ring theory, a branch of abstract algebra, a _____ is an ideal I in a ring R that is generated by a single element a of R.

More specifically:

- a left _____ of R is a subset of R of the form Ra := {ra : r in R};
- a right _____ is a subset of the form aR := {ar : r in R};
- a two-sided _____ is a subset of the form RaR := {$r_1 a s_1$ + ... + $r_n a s_n$: $r_1, s_1, ..., r_n, s_n$ in R}.

If R is a commutative ring, then the above three notions are all the same. In that case, it is common to write the ideal generated by a as (a.)

Not all ideals are principal.

a. Radical of an ideal
b. Radical of an ring
c. Primitive ideal
d. Principal ideal

37. In abstract algebra, a _____ i.e., can be generated by a single element. More generally, a principal ring is a nonzero commutative ring whose ideals are principal, although some authors (e.g., Bourbaki) refers to Principal ideal domains as principal rings. The distinction being that a principal ideal ring may have zero divisors whereas a _____ cannot.

a. Discrete valuation
b. Nilradical
c. Principal ideal domain
d. Minimal prime

38. In abstract algebra, the _____ is a construction which combines several modules into a new, larger module. The result of the direct summation of modules is the 'smallest general' module which contains the given modules as subspaces. This is an example of a coproduct.

a. Schmidt decomposition
b. Finite dimensional von Neumann algebra
c. Frame
d. Direct sum

39. In mathematics, a _____ is a flat surface. Planes can arise as subspaces of some higher dimensional space, as with the walls of a room, or they may enjoy an independent existence in their own right, as in the setting of Euclidean geometry

a. -equivalence
b. -module
c. Similarity
d. Plane

40. In linear algebra, two vectors in an inner product space are _____ if they are orthogonal and both of unit length. A set of vectors form an _____ set if all vectors in the set are mutually orthogonal and all of unit length. An _____ set which forms a basis is called an _____ basis.
   a. Invertible matrix
   b. Overdetermined
   c. Elementary matrix
   d. Orthonormal

41. In mathematics, an _____ of an inner product space V (i.e., a vector space with an inner product), is a set of mutually orthogonal vectors of magnitude 1 (unit vectors) that span the space when infinite linear combinations are allowed. (In some contexts, especially in linear algebra, the concept of basis (linear algebra) means a set of vectors that span a space when only finite linear combinations are allowed.) Such an infinite linear combination is an infinite series, and the concept of convergence relied upon is defined in terms of the space's inner product.
   a. Orientation
   b. Eigendecomposition
   c. Overdetermined
   d. Orthonormal basis

42. _____ is definite, that is, has a real value with the same sign (positive or negative) for all non-zero x. According to that sign, B is called positive definite or _____. If Q takes both positive and negative values, the bilinear form B is called indefinite.
   a. -module
   b. -equivalence
   c. 2-bridge knot
   d. Negative definite

43. In mathematics, a _____ is a homogeneous polynomial of degree two in a number of variables. For example,

$$4x^2 + 2xy - 3y^2$$

is a _____ in the variables x and y.

Quadratic forms are central objects in mathematics, occurring for instance in number theory, geometry (Riemannian metric), topology (intersection forms on homology), and Lie theory (the Killing form.)

   a. Rank
   b. Partial trace
   c. Homogeneous coordinates
   d. Quadratic form

44. In the mathematical field of knot theory, the _____ of a knot is a knot invariant obtained from a quadratic form associated to a Seifert surface. If F is a Seifert surface of a knot, then the homology group H_1(F, Z/2Z) has a quadratic form whose value is the number of full twists mod 2 in a neighborhood of an imbedded circle representing an element of the homology group. The _____ of this quadratic form is the _____ of the knot.
   a. Average crossing number
   b. Unknotting problem
   c. Invertible knot
   d. Arf invariant

45. The _____ and descending chain condition (DCC) are finiteness properties satisfied by certain algebraic structures, most importantly, ideals in a commutative ring. These conditions played an important role in the development of the structure theory of commutative rings in the works of David Hilbert, Emmy Noether, and Emil Artin. The conditions themselves can be stated in an abstract form, so that they make sense for any partially ordered set.

a. Atomic domain
c. Integral

b. Invariant polynomial
d. Ascending chain condition

46. In algebraic topology, a simplicial k-_____ is a formal linear combination of k-simplices.

Integration is defined on chains by taking the linear combination of integrals over the simplices in the _____ with coefficients typically integers. The set of all k-chains forms a group and the sequence of these groups is called a _____ complex.

a. Combinatorial topology
c. Bockstein homomorphism

b. Chain
d. Tesseract

47. In mathematics, there are several meanings of _____ depending on the subject.

A _____, usually denoted by ° (the _____ symbol), is a measurement of plane angle, representing $1/360$ of a full rotation. When that angle is with respect to a reference meridian, it indicates a location along a great circle of a sphere, such as Earth, Mars, or the celestial sphere.

a. Symmetric difference
c. Degree

b. Relation algebra
d. Median algebra

48. In mathematics, in particular abstract algebra, a _____ is an algebra over a field (or commutative ring) with an extra piece of structure, known as a gradation (or grading.)

A graded ring A is a ring that has a direct sum decomposition into (abelian) additive groups

$$A = \bigoplus_{n \in \mathbb{N}} A_n = A_0 \oplus A_1 \oplus A_2 \oplus \cdots$$

such that the ring multiplication maps

$$A_s \times A_r \to A_{s+r}.$$

Explicitly this means that

$$x \in A_s, y \in A_r \implies xy \in A_{s+r}$$

and so

$$A_s A_r \subseteq A_{s+r}.$$

Elements of A_n are known as homogeneous elements of degree n. An ideal or other subset $\mathfrak{a} \subset A$ is homogeneous if for every element a $\in \mathfrak{a}$, the homogeneous parts of a are also contained in $\mathfrak{a}$.

If I is a homogeneous ideal in A, then A / I is also a graded ring, and has decomposition

$$A/I = \bigoplus_{n \in \mathbb{N}} (A_n + I)/I$$

a. Bifundamental representation
b. Noetherian module
c. Semisimple
d. Graded algebra

49. A _____ is a symbol that stands for a value that may vary; the term usually occurs in opposition to constant, which is a symbol for a non-varying value, i.e. completely fixed or fixed in the context of use. The concepts of constants and variables are fundamental to all modern mathematics, science, engineering, and computer programming.

Much of the basic theory for which we use variables today, such as school geometry and algebra, was developed thousands of years ago, but the use of symbolic formulae and variables is only several hundreds of years old.

a. 2-bridge knot
b. -module
c. -equivalence
d. Variable

50. In mathematics, the _____ of a vector space V, denoted T(V) or T'(V), is the algebra of tensors on V (of any rank) with multiplication being the tensor product. It is the free algebra on V, in the sense of being left adjoint to the forgetful functor from algebras to vector spaces: it is the 'most general' algebra containing V, in the sense of the corresponding universal property

The _____ also has a coalgebra structure.

a. Tensor algebra
b. Monster vertex algebra
c. Normed division algebra
d. Free algebra

51. In mathematics, especially in the area of abstract algebra known as ring theory, a _____ is the noncommutative analogue of a polynomial ring (which may be regarded as a free commutative algebra.)

For R a commutative ring, the free (associative, unital) algebra on n indeterminates, $\{X_1, ..., X_n\}$, is the ring spanned by all sums of products of the variables. This ring is denoted R<$X_1, ..., X_n$>.

a. Free algebra
b. Semisimple
c. Regular p-group
d. Capable

Chapter 9. Advanced Linear Algebra

52. In mathematics, especially in the field of abstract algebra, a _____ is a ring formed from the set of polynomials in one or more variables with coefficients in another ring. Polynomial rings have influenced much of mathematics, from the Hilbert basis theorem, to the construction of splitting fields, and to the understanding of a linear operator. Many important conjectures, such as Serre's conjecture, have influenced the study of other rings, and have influenced even the definition of other rings, such as group rings and rings of formal power series.

a. Polynomial ring
b. Nilradical
c. Dedekind domain
d. Commutative ring

53. In mathematics, a _____ is a type of algebraic structure. There is some variation among mathematicians as to exactly what properties a _____ is required to have, as described in detail below. However, commonly a _____ is defined as a set together with two binary operations (usually called addition and multiplication), where each operation combines two elements to form a third element.

a. -module
b. 2-bridge knot
c. Ring
d. -equivalence

54. In mathematics, a polynomial P(X) is _____ over a field K if all of its irreducible factors have distinct roots in an algebraic closure of K - that is each irreducible factor of P(X) has distinct linear factors in some large enough field extension. There is, however, another, non-equivalent definition of separability. It says that P is _____ if and only if it is coprime to its formal derivative P'.

a. Global field
b. Transcendence degree
c. Field of fractions
d. Separable

55. In ring theory and related areas of mathematics a _____ over a field K is a finite-dimensional associative algebra A, which is simple, and for which the center is exactly K. In other words, any simple algebra is a _____ over its center.

For example, the complex numbers C form a _____ over themselves, but not over the real numbers R (the center of C is all of C, not just R.) The quaternions H form a 4 dimensional _____ over R.

a. Lewis Carroll identity
b. Representation rigid
c. Metacyclic group
d. Central simple algebra

56. In mathematics, especially in elementary arithmetic, _____ is an arithmetic operation which is the inverse of multiplication.

Specifically, if c times b equals a, written:

$$c \times b = a$$

where b is not zero, then a divided by b equals c, written:

$$\frac{a}{b} = c$$

For instance,

$$\frac{6}{3} = 2$$

since

$$2 \times 3 = 6.$$

In the above expression, a is called the dividend, b the divisor and c the quotient.

a. Division
b. -equivalence
c. 2-bridge knot
d. -module

57. In the field of mathematics called abstract algebra, a _____ is, roughly speaking, an algebra over a field in which division is possible.

Formally, we start with an algebra D over a field, and assume that D does not just consist of its zero element. We call D a _____ if for any element a in D and any non-zero element b in D there exists precisely one element x in D with a = bx and precisely one element y in D such that a = yb.

a. Frobenius algebra
b. Garside element
c. Division algebra
d. Depth

58. In mathematics, the term _____ is used to describe an algebraic structures which in some sense cannot be divided by a smaller structure of the same type. Put another way, an algebraic structure is _____ if the kernel of every homomorphism is either the whole structure or a single element. Some examples are:

- A group is called a _____ group if it does not contain a non-trivial proper normal subgroup.
- A ring is called a _____ ring if it does not contain a non-trivial two sided ideal.
- A module is called a _____ module if does not contain a non-trivial submodule.
- An algebra is called a _____ algebra if does not contain a non-trivial two sided ideal.

The general pattern is that the structure admits no non-trivial congruence relations.

a. Commutativity
b. Simple
c. Linear combinations
d. Polarization identity

59. In mathematics and theoretical physics, a _____ is a Z_2-graded algebra. That is, it is an algebra over a commutative ring or field with a decomposition into 'even' and 'odd' pieces and a multiplication operator that respects the grading.

The prefix super- comes from the theory of supersymmetry in theoretical physics.

a. Dunkl operator	b. Representation rigid
c. Superalgebra	d. Birational invariant

60. In group theory, the _____ and normalizer of a subset S of a group G are subgroups of G which have a restricted action on the elements of S and S as a whole, respectively. These subgroups provide insight into the structure of G.

The _____ of an element a of a group G (written as $C_G(a)$) is the set of elements of G which commute with a; in other words, $C_G(a) = \{x \in G : xa = ax\}$.

a. HN group	b. Class automorphism
c. Centralizer	d. Stallings' theorem about ends of groups

61. In abstract algebra, a _____ is an algebraic structure with notions of addition, subtraction, multiplication and division, satisfying certain axioms. The most commonly used fields are the _____ of real numbers, the _____ of complex numbers, and the _____ of rational numbers, but there are also finite fields, fields of functions, various algebraic number fields, p-adic fields, and so forth.

Any _____ may be used as the scalars for a vector space, which is the standard general context for linear algebra.

a. Tensor product of fields	b. Generic polynomial
c. Field	d. Separable

62. In abstract algebra, the _____ of a polynomial P(X) over a given field K is a field extension L of K, over which P factorizes into linear factors

$X - a_i$,

and such that the a_i generate L over K. It can be shown that such splitting fields exist, and are unique up to isomorphism; the amount of freedom in that isomorphism is known to be the Galois group of P.

For an example if K is the rational number field Q and

$P = X^3 - 2$,

then a _____ L will contain a primitive cube root of unity, as well as a cube root of 2. Thus

$$L = \mathbb{Q}(\sqrt[3]{2}, \omega_2) = \{a + b\omega_2 + c\sqrt[3]{2} + d\sqrt[3]{2}\omega_2 + e\sqrt[3]{2}^2 + f\sqrt[3]{2}^2\omega_2 \mid a, b, c, d, e, f \in \mathbb{Q}\}$$

where

$$\omega_1 = 1,$$
$$\omega_2 = -\frac{1}{2} + \frac{\sqrt{3}}{2}i,$$ and
$$\omega_3 = -\frac{1}{2} - \frac{\sqrt{3}}{2}i$$

are the cubic roots of unity.

   a. Formally real field
   b. Splitting field
   c. Fundamental theorem of Galois theory
   d. Field of fractions

63. In abstract algebra, a _____ is a ring in which division is possible. More formally, a ring with $0 \neq 1$ is a _____ if every non-zero element a has a multiplicative inverse Division rings differ from fields only in that their multiplication is not required to be commutative.
   a. Square-free
   b. Local ring
   c. Division ring
   d. Ring homomorphism

64. In mathematics, more specifically in abstract algebra, the _____, proved by Ferdinand Georg Frobenius in 1877, characterizes the finite dimensional associative division algebras over the real numbers. The theorem proves that the only associative division algebra which is not commutative over the real numbers is the quaternions.

If D is a finite dimensional division algebra over the real numbers R then one of the following cases holds

- D = R
- D = C (complex numbers)
- D = H (quaternions.)

The main ingredients for the following proof are the Cayley-Hamilton Theorem and the Fundamental theorem of algebra.

We can consider D as a finite-dimensional R-vector space.

   a. Tensor algebra
   b. Frobenius theorem
   c. Garside element
   d. Dixmier conjecture

65. In the various branches of mathematics that fall under the heading of abstract algebra, the _____ of a homomorphism measures the degree to which the homomorphism fails to be injective. An important special case is the _____ of a matrix, also called the null space.

The definition of _____ takes various forms in various contexts.

Chapter 9. Advanced Linear Algebra

a. Monomial basis
b. Kernel
c. Completing the square
d. K-theory

66. In mathematics, the _____ arose out of an attempt to classify division algebras over a given field K. It is an abelian group with elements equivalence classes of Azumaya algebras (finite dimensional simple division algebras over K, such that the center is exactly K.) The group is named for the algebraist Richard Brauer.

A central simple algebra (CSA) over a field K is a finite-dimensional associative K-algebra A, which is a simple ring, and for which the center is exactly K. For example, the complex numbers C form a CSA over themselves, but not over R (the center is C itself, hence too large to be CSA over R.)

a. Brauer group
b. Division ring
c. Matrix ring
d. Zero ring

67. The _____ is often met for the first time as an operation on a single real function of a single real variable. One of the simplest settings for generalizations is to vector valued functions of several variables (most often the domain forms a vector space as well.) This is the field of multivariable calculus.

a. 2-bridge knot
b. -module
c. -equivalence
d. Derivative

68. In mathematics, the _____ S(V) (also denoted Sym(V)) on a vector space V over a field K is the free commutative unital associative K-algebra containing V.

It corresponds to polynomials with indeterminates in V, without choosing coordinates. The dual, S(V*) corresponds to polynomials on V.

a. -module
b. 2-bridge knot
c. -equivalence
d. Symmetric algebra

69. In mathematics, _____ are a type of associative algebra. They can be thought of as one of the possible generalizations of the complex numbers and quaternions. The theory of _____ is intimately connected with the theory of quadratic forms and orthogonal transformations.

a. Clifford algebras
b. Dirac algebra
c. Twistor theory
d. Clifford bundle

70. In algebra, a _____ is a function depending on n that associates a scalar, det(A), to an n×n square matrix A. The fundamental geometric meaning of a _____ is a scale factor for measure when A is regarded as a linear transformation. Determinants are important both in calculus, where they enter the substitution rule for several variables, and in multilinear algebra.

For a fixed nonnegative integer n, there is a unique _____ function for the n×n matrices over any commutative ring R. In particular, this function exists when R is the field of real or complex numbers.

a. Leibniz formula
b. Pfaffian
c. Functional determinant
d. Determinant

71. In linear algebra, a _____ of a matrix A is the determinant of some smaller square matrix, cut down from A by removing one or more of its rows or columns. Minors obtained by removing just one row and one column from square matrices (first minors) are required for calculating matrix cofactors, which in turn are useful for computing both the determinant and inverse of square matrices.

- a. Purification
- b. Supergroup
- c. Rng
- d. Minor

72. In mathematics, a _____ is a matrix formed by selecting certain rows and columns from a bigger matrix. That is, as an array, it is cut down to those entries constrained by row and column.

For example

$$\mathbf{A} = \begin{bmatrix} a_{11} & a_{12} & a_{13} & a_{14} \\ a_{21} & a_{22} & a_{23} & a_{24} \\ a_{31} & a_{32} & a_{33} & a_{34} \end{bmatrix}.$$

Then

$$\mathbf{A}[1,2;1,3,4] = \begin{bmatrix} a_{11} & a_{13} & a_{14} \\ a_{21} & a_{23} & a_{24} \end{bmatrix}$$

is a _____ of A formed by rows 1,2 and columns 1,3,4.

- a. Quasideterminant
- b. Lie product formula
- c. Smith normal form
- d. Submatrix

73. In linear algebra, the _____ of the determinant of an n × n square matrix B expresses the determinant $|B|$ as a sum of n determinants of (n-1) × (n-1) sub-matrices of B. There are n^2 such expressions, one for each row and column of B. The _____ is of theoretical interest as one of several ways to view the determinant, as well as of practical use in determinant computation.

Define the i,j minor matrix M_{ij} of B as the (n-1) × (n-1) matrix that results from deleting the i-th row and the j-th column of B, and $C_{i,j}$ the cofactor of B as

$$C_{ij} = (-1)^{i+j} |M_{ij}|.$$

Then the _____ is given by the following

Theorem Suppose B = (b_{ij}) is an n × n matrix and i,j ∈ {1, 2, ...,n}.

Then the determinant

$$|B| = b_{i1}C_{i1} + b_{i2}C_{i2} + \cdots + b_{in}C_{in}$$
$$= b_{1j}C_{1j} + b_{2j}C_{2j} + \cdots + b_{nj}C_{nj}.$$

Consider the matrix

$$B = \begin{bmatrix} 1 & 2 & 3 \\ 4 & 5 & 6 \\ 7 & 8 & 9 \end{bmatrix}.$$

The determinant of this matrix can be computed by using the _____ along the first row:

$$|B| = 1 \cdot \begin{vmatrix} 5 & 6 \\ 8 & 9 \end{vmatrix} - 2 \cdot \begin{vmatrix} 4 & 6 \\ 7 & 9 \end{vmatrix} + 3 \cdot \begin{vmatrix} 4 & 5 \\ 7 & 8 \end{vmatrix}$$

$$= 1 \cdot (-3) - 2 \cdot (-6) + 3 \cdot (-3) = 0.$$

Alternatively, _____ along the second column yields

$$|B| = -2 \cdot \begin{vmatrix} 4 & 6 \\ 7 & 9 \end{vmatrix} + 5 \cdot \begin{vmatrix} 1 & 3 \\ 7 & 9 \end{vmatrix} - 8 \cdot \begin{vmatrix} 1 & 3 \\ 4 & 6 \end{vmatrix}$$

$$= -2 \cdot (-6) + 5 \cdot (-12) - 8 \cdot (-6) = 0.$$

It is easy to see that the result is correct: the matrix is singular because the sum of its first and third column is twice the second column, and hence its determinant is zero.

a. Square root of a matrix
c. Matrix function
b. Matrix decomposition
d. Laplace expansion

74. In mathematics, an _____ of a product of sums expresses it as a sum of products by using the fact that multiplication distributes over addition. Expansions of polynomials are obtained by multiplying together their factors, which results in a sum of terms with variables raised to different degrees.

To multiply two factors, each term of the first factor must be multiplied by each term of the other factor.

a. Equipotential surfaces
c. Expansion
b. Ordered vector space
d. Analytic subgroup

Chapter 9. Advanced Linear Algebra

75. In linear algebra, the _____ describes a particular construction that is useful for calculating both the determinant and inverse of square matrices. Specifically the _____ of the (i, j) entry of a matrix, also known as the (i, j) _____ of that matrix, is the signed minor of that entry.

Finding the minors of a matrix A is a multi-step process:

1. Choose an entry a_{ij} from the matrix.
2. Cross out the entries that lie in the corresponding row i and column j.
3. Rewrite the matrix without the marked entries.
4. Obtain the determinant M_{ij} of this new matrix.

M_{ij} is termed the minor for entry a_{ij}.

If i + j is an even number, the _____ C_{ij} of a_{ij} coincides with its minor:

$$C_{ij} = M_{ij}.$$

Otherwise, it is equal to the additive inverse of its minor:

$$C_{ij} = -M_{ij}.$$

If A is a square matrix, then the minor of its entry a_{ij}, also known as the i,j, or (i,j), or (i,j)th minor of A, is denoted by M_{ij} and is defined to be the determinant of the submatrix obtained by removing from A its i-th row and j-th column.

a. Resolvent set
b. Complex structure
c. Cofactor
d. Coefficient matrix

76. Let S be a set with a binary operation * . If e is an identity element of (S, *) and a * b = e, then a is called a _____ of b and b is called a right inverse of a. If an element x is both a _____ and a right inverse of y, then x is called a two-sided inverse, or simply an inverse, of y.

a. -module
b. Left inverse
c. 2-bridge knot
d. -equivalence

77. Matrix inversion is the process of finding the matrix B that satisfies the prior equation for a given _____ A.

a. Independent equation
b. Overdetermined
c. Orientation
d. Invertible matrix

78. In linear algebra, the _____ of an n-by-n square matrix A is defined to be the sum of the elements on the main diagonal (the diagonal from the upper left to the lower right) of A, i.e.,

$$\text{tr}(A) = a_{11} + a_{22} + \cdots + a_{nn} = \sum_{i=1}^{n} a_{ii}$$

where a_{ij} represents the entry on the ith row and jth column of A. Equivalently, the _____ of a matrix is the sum of its eigenvalues, making it an invariant with respect to a change of basis. This characterization can be used to define the _____ for a linear operator in general.

Note that the _____ is only defined for a square matrix (i.e. n×n.)

a. Coefficient matrix
c. Dot product

b. Trace
d. Defective matrix

79. In linear algebra, a _____ is a matrix with the terms of a geometric progression in each row, i.e., an m × n matrix

$$V = \begin{bmatrix} 1 & \alpha_1 & \alpha_1^2 & \cdots & \alpha_1^{n-1} \\ 1 & \alpha_2 & \alpha_2^2 & \cdots & \alpha_2^{n-1} \\ 1 & \alpha_3 & \alpha_3^2 & \cdots & \alpha_3^{n-1} \\ \vdots & \vdots & \vdots & \ddots & \vdots \\ 1 & \alpha_m & \alpha_m^2 & \cdots & \alpha_m^{n-1} \end{bmatrix}$$

or

$$V_{i,j} = \alpha_i^{j-1}$$

for all indices i and j. (Some authors use the transpose of the above matrix.)

The determinant of a square _____ can be expressed as:

$$\det(V) = \prod_{1 \leq i < j \leq n} (\alpha_j - \alpha_i).$$

This is called the Vandermonde determinant or Vandermonde polynomial.

a. Vandermonde matrix
c. Diagonalizable matrix

b. Zero matrix
d. Pascal matrix

80. In mathematics, an _____ is a vector space (or more generally, a module) which also allows the multiplication of vectors in a distributive and associative manner. They are thus special algebras.

An _____ A over a field K is defined to be a vector space over K together with a K-bilinear multiplication A x A → A (where the image of (x,y) is written as xy) such that the associative law holds:

- (x y) z = x (y z) for all x, y and z in A.

The bilinearity of the multiplication can be expressed as

- (x + y) z = x z + y z for all x, y, z in A,
- x (y + z) = x y + x z for all x, y, z in A,
- a (x y) = (a x) y = x (a y) for all x, y in A and a in K.

If A contains an identity element, i.e. an element 1 such that 1x = x1 = x for all x in A, then we call A an _____ with one or a unital (or unitary) _____.

a. Algebra over a field
b. Affine representation
c. Associative algebra
d. Elementary amenable group

81. In mathematics the _____ is a property that a binary operation can satisfy which determines how the order of evaluation behaves for the given operation. Unlike for associative operations, order of evaluation is significant for operations satisfying _____.

A binary operation * on a set S possessing a commutative binary operation +, satisfies the _____ if

$$a * (b * c) + c * (a * b) + b * (c * a) = 0 \quad \forall a, b, c \in S.$$

In a Lie algebra, the objects that obey the _____ are infinitesimal motions.

a. Knizhnik-Zamolodchikov equations
b. Lie ring
c. Jacobi identity
d. Nilpotent orbit

82. In mathematics, especially in the fields of group theory and Lie theory, a _____ is a kind of normal series of subgroups or Lie subalgebras, expressing the idea that the commutator is nearly trivial. For groups, this is an explicit expression that the group is a nilpotent group, and for matrix rings, this is an explicit expression that in some basis the matrix ring consists entirely of upper triangular matrices with constant diagonal

a. Central series
b. Rank of a group
c. Fitting length
d. Quaternion group

83. A _____ between two algebras over a field K, A and B, is a map $F : A \to B$ such that for all k in K and x,y in A,

- F(kx) = kF(x)

- F(x + y) = F(x) + F(y)

- F(xy) = F(x)F(y)

If F is bijective then F is said to be an isomorphism between A and B.

Let A = K[x] be the set of all polynomials over a field K and B be the set of all polynomial functions over K. Both A and B are algebras over K given by the standard multiplication and addition of polynomials and functions, respectively. We can map each f in A to $\hat{f}$ in B by the rule $\hat{f}(t) = f(t)$. A routine check shows that the mapping $f \mapsto \hat{f}$ is a _____ of the algebras A and B. If K is a finite field then let

$$p(x) = \Pi_{t \in K}(x - t).$$

p is a nonzero polynomial in K[x], however $p(t) = 0$ for all t in K, so $\hat{p} = 0$ is the zero function and the algebras are not isomorphic.

a. Tensor algebra
c. Tensor product of algebras
b. Frobenius matrix
d. Homomorphism

Chapter 10. Homology

1. In mathematics (especially algebraic topology and abstract algebra), _____ is a certain general procedure to associate a sequence of abelian groups or modules with a given mathematical object such as a topological space or a group. See _____ theory for more background, or singular _____ for a concrete version for topological spaces, or group cohomology for a concrete version for groups.

   For a topological space, the _____ groups are generally much easier to compute than the homotopy groups, and consequently one usually will have an easier time working with _____ to aid in the classification of spaces.

   - a. Morse homology
   - b. Cohomology ring
   - c. Cap product
   - d. Homology

2. In mathematics, the _____ of a ring R, often denoted char(R), is defined to be the smallest number of times one must add the ring's multiplicative identity element (1) to itself to get the additive identity element (0); the ring is said to have _____ zero if this repeated sum never reaches the additive identity. That is, char(R) is the smallest positive number n such that

$$\underbrace{1 + \cdots + 1}_{n \text{ summands}} = 0$$

   if such a number n exists, and 0 otherwise. The _____ may also be taken to be the exponent of the ring's additive group, that is, the smallest positive n such that

$$\underbrace{a + \cdots + a}_{n \text{ summands}} = 0$$

   for every element a of the ring (again, if n exists; otherwise zero.)

   - a. Coherent ring
   - b. Free ideal ring
   - c. Hereditary
   - d. Characteristic

3. A _____ is a set G closed under a binary operation · satisfying the following 3 axioms:

   - Associativity: For all a, b and c in G, (a · b) · c = a · (b · c.)
   - Identity element: There exists an e∈G such that for all a in G, e · a = a · e = a.
   - Inverse element: For each a in G, there is an element b in G such that a · b = b · a = e, where e is an identity element.

   Basic examples for groups are the integers Z with addition operation, or rational numbers without zero Q{0} with multiplication. More generally, for any ring R, the units in R form a multiplicative _____ Groups include, however, much more general structures than the above.

   - a. Product of group subsets
   - b. Nilpotent group
   - c. Grigorchuk group
   - d. Group

Chapter 10. Homology

4. In mathematics, an _____ is an isomorphism from a mathematical object to itself. It is, in some sense, a symmetry of the object, and a way of mapping the object to itself while preserving all of its structure. The set of all automorphisms of an object forms a group, called the _____ group.
   - a. Endomorphism
   - b. Epimorphism
   - c. ADE classification
   - d. Automorphism

5. In abstract algebra, a _____ is an algebraic structure with notions of addition, subtraction, multiplication and division, satisfying certain axioms. The most commonly used fields are the _____ of real numbers, the _____ of complex numbers, and the _____ of rational numbers, but there are also finite fields, fields of functions, various algebraic number fields, p-adic fields, and so forth.

   Any _____ may be used as the scalars for a vector space, which is the standard general context for linear algebra.

   - a. Tensor product of fields
   - b. Generic polynomial
   - c. Separable
   - d. Field

6. In discrete mathematics and predominantly in set theory, a _____ is a concept used in comparisons of sets to refer to the unique values of one set in relation to another. The terms 'absolute' and 'relative' _____ refer to more specific applications of the concept, with universal complements referring to elements unique to the universal set and the latter referring to the unique elements of one set in relation to another. In this image, the universal set is represented by the border of the image, and the set A as a disc.
   - a. -module
   - b. Complement
   - c. Pointed set
   - d. -equivalence

7. In mathematics, especially in the area of abstract algebra known as ring theory, a _____ is a ring with $0 \neq 1$ such that $ab = 0$ implies that either $a = 0$ or $b = 0$ (the zero-product property.) That is, it is a nontrivial ring without left or right zero divisors. A commutative _____ is called an integral _____.
   - a. Coherent ring
   - b. Subring
   - c. Partially-ordered ring
   - d. Domain

8. In mathematics, _____ or factoring is the decomposition of an object ' href='/wiki/Matrix_(mathematics)'>matrix) into a product of other objects, or factors, which when multiplied together give the original. For example, the number 15 factors into primes as 3 × 5, and the polynomial $x^2 - 4$ factors as $(x - 2)(x + 2)$. In all cases, a product of simpler objects is obtained.
   - a. 2-bridge knot
   - b. -module
   - c. -equivalence
   - d. Factorization

9. In mathematics, a _____ is, roughly speaking, a commutative ring in which every element, with special exceptions, can be uniquely written as a product of prime elements, analogous to the fundamental theorem of arithmetic for the integers. Unique factorization domains are sometimes called factorial rings, following the terminology of Bourbaki.

Note that unique factorization domains appear in the following chain of class inclusions:

- Commutative rings ⊃ integral domains ⊃ unique factorization domains ⊃ principal ideal domains ⊃ Euclidean domains ⊃ fields

a. Unique factorization domain
b. Absorption law
c. Unit ring
d. Isomorphism class

10. In mathematics, the _____ of degree n, denoted SU(n), is the group of n×n unitary matrices with determinant 1. The group operation is that of matrix multiplication. The _____ is a subgroup of the unitary group U(n), consisting of all n×n unitary matrices, which is itself a subgroup of the general linear group GL(n, C.)

a. Cartan subgroup
b. Simple Lie group
c. Bruhat decomposition
d. Special unitary group

11. In mathematics, specifically in algebraic topology, _____ is a general term for a sequence of abelian groups defined from a cochain complex. That is, _____ is defined as the abstract study of cochains, cocycles, and coboundaries. _____ can be viewed as a method of assigning algebraic invariants to a topological space that has a more refined algebraic structure than does homology.

a. Cohomology
b. Classifying space
c. Topological modular forms
d. Morava K-theory

12. In mathematics, there are several meanings of _____ depending on the subject.

A _____, usually denoted by ° (the _____ symbol), is a measurement of plane angle, representing $1/360$ of a full rotation. When that angle is with respect to a reference meridian, it indicates a location along a great circle of a sphere, such as Earth , Mars, or the celestial sphere.

a. Symmetric difference
b. Relation algebra
c. Degree
d. Median algebra

13. In abstract algebra, a _____ is a function on an algebra which generalizes certain features of the derivative operator. Specifically, given an algebra A over a ring or a field F, an F-_____ is an F-linear map D: A → A that satisfies Leibniz's law:

D(ab) = (Da)b + a(Db.)

More generally, an F-linear map D of A into an A-module M, satisfying the Leibniz law is also called a _____. The collection of all F-derivations of A to itself is denoted by Der$_F$(A.)

a. Pincherle derivative
b. Derivation
c. Transcendental function
d. Differential algebras

Chapter 10. Homology

14. A _____ between two algebras over a field K, A and B, is a map $F : A \to B$ such that for all k in K and x,y in A,

- F(kx) = kF(x)

- F(x + y) = F(x) + F(y)

- F(xy) = F(x)F(y)

If F is bijective then F is said to be an isomorphism between A and B.

Let A = K[x] be the set of all polynomials over a field K and B be the set of all polynomial functions over K. Both A and B are algebras over K given by the standard multiplication and addition of polynomials and functions, respectively. We can map each f in A to $\hat{f}$ in B by the rule $\hat{f}(t) = f(t)$. A routine check shows that the mapping $f \mapsto \hat{f}$ is a _____ of the algebras A and B. If K is a finite field then let

$$p(x) = \Pi_{t \in K}(x - t).$$

p is a nonzero polynomial in K[x], however $p(t) = 0$ for all t in K, so $\hat{p} = 0$ is the zero function and the algebras are not isomorphic.

a. Homomorphism
c. Tensor algebra
b. Tensor product of algebras
d. Frobenius matrix

15. A _____ is a symbol that stands for a value that may vary; the term usually occurs in opposition to constant, which is a symbol for a non-varying value, i.e. completely fixed or fixed in the context of use. The concepts of constants and variables are fundamental to all modern mathematics, science, engineering, and computer programming.

Much of the basic theory for which we use variables today, such as school geometry and algebra, was developed thousands of years ago, but the use of symbolic formulae and variables is only several hundreds of years old.

a. Variable
c. 2-bridge knot
b. -equivalence
d. -module

16. _____, in mathematics, are a non-commutative number system that extends the complex numbers. The _____ were first described by Irish mathematician Sir William Rowan Hamilton in 1843 and applied to mechanics in three-dimensional space. They find uses in both theoretical and applied mathematics, in particular for calculations involving three-dimensional rotations , such as in 3D computer graphics, although they have been superseded in many applications by vectors and matrices.

a. Split-quaternions
c. Generalized quaternion interpolation
b. Split-biquaternion
d. Quaternions

17. In mathematics, particularly in abstract algebra and homological algebra, a _____ is a sequence which is used to describe the structure of a module.

Chapter 10. Homology

If the modules involved in the sequence have a property P then one speaks of a P _____: for example, a flat _____, a free _____, an injective _____, a projective _____ and so on.

Given a module M over a ring R, a _____ of M is an exact sequence (possibly infinite) of modules

$\cdots \to E_n \to \cdots \to E_2 \to E_1 \to E_0 \to M \to 0,$

with all the E_i modules over R. The _____ is said to be finite if the sequence of E_i is zero from some point onwards.

    a. Projective representation   b. Homological algebra
    c. Hodge structure   d. Resolution

18. In mathematics, a _____ is an algebraic structure whose main use is in studying geometric objects such as Lie groups and differentiable manifolds. Lie algebras were introduced to study the concept of infinitesimal transformations. The term '_____') was introduced by Hermann Weyl in the 1930s.

    a. Weyl group   b. Maximal torus
    c. Lorentz group   d. Lie algebra

19. In algebraic topology, a simplicial k-_____ is a formal linear combination of k-simplices.

Integration is defined on chains by taking the linear combination of integrals over the simplices in the _____ with coefficients typically integers. The set of all k-chains forms a group and the sequence of these groups is called a _____ complex.

    a. Bockstein homomorphism   b. Tesseract
    c. Combinatorial topology   d. Chain

20. In mathematics, and in particular in group theory, a _____ is a permutation of the elements of some set X which maps the elements of some subset S to each other in a cyclic fashion, while fixing (i.e., mapping to themselves) all other elements. The set S is called the orbit of the _____.

A permutation of a set X, which is a bijective function $\sigma : X \to X$, is called a _____ if the action on X of the subgroup generated by σ has exactly one orbit with more than a single element.

    a. Nested radical   b. Cycle
    c. Continuant   d. Definition .

21. The _____ and descending chain condition (DCC) are finiteness properties satisfied by certain algebraic structures, most importantly, ideals in a commutative ring. These conditions played an important role in the development of the structure theory of commutative rings in the works of David Hilbert, Emmy Noether, and Emil Artin. The conditions themselves can be stated in an abstract form, so that they make sense for any partially ordered set.

Chapter 10. Homology

a. Invariant polynomial
b. Integral
c. Ascending chain condition
d. Atomic domain

22. In topology, two continuous functions from one topological space to another are called _____ if one can be 'continuously deformed' into the other, such a deformation being called a homotopy between the two functions. An outstanding use of homotopy is the definition of homotopy groups and cohomotopy groups, important invariants in algebraic topology.

In practice, there are technical difficulties in using homotopies with certain pathological spaces.

a. Model structure
b. Homotopic
c. Stunted projective space
d. Puppe sequence

23. In topology, two continuous functions from one topological space to another are called homotopic if one can be 'continuously deformed' into the other, such a deformation being called a _____ between the two functions. An outstanding use of _____ is the definition of _____ groups and cohomotopy groups, important invariants in algebraic topology.

In practice, there are technical difficulties in using homotopies with certain pathological spaces.

a. Simple-homotopy equivalence
b. Homotopy
c. Freudenthal suspension theorem
d. J-homomorphism

24. A _____ is one of the basic shapes of geometry: a polygon with three corners or vertices and three sides or edges which are line segments. A _____ with vertices A, B, and C is denoted ABC.

In Euclidean geometry any three non-collinear points determine a unique _____ and a unique plane (i.e. a two-dimensional Euclidean space.)

a. -equivalence
b. Triangle
c. 2-bridge knot
d. -module

25. In mathematics, the _____ of a vector space V is the cardinality (i.e. the number of vectors) of a basis of V. It is sometimes called Hamel _____ or algebraic _____ to distinguish it from other types of _____. All bases of a vector space have equal cardinality and so the _____ of a vector space is uniquely defined. The _____ of the vector space V over the field F can be written as $\dim_F(V)$ or as [V : F], read '_____ of V over F'.

a. Cofactor
b. Dual basis
c. Partial trace
d. Dimension

26. In abstract algebra, the concept of a _____ over a ring is a generalization of the notion of vector space, where instead of requiring the scalars to lie in a field, the 'scalars' may lie in an arbitrary ring. Modules also generalize the notion of abelian groups, which are modules over $\mathbb{Z}$.

Thus, a _____, like a vector space, is an additive abelian group; a product is defined between elements of the ring and elements of the _____, and this multiplication is associative (when used with the multiplication in the ring) and distributive.

a. Goodman-Nguyen-van Fraassen algebra
c. Near-field
b. Semigroupoid
d. Module

27. In mathematics, a _____ is a constant multiplicative factor of a certain object. For example, in the expression $9x^2$, the _____ of x^2 is 9.

The object can be such things as a variable, a vector, a function, etc.

a. Tschirnhaus transformation
c. Constant term
b. Vandermonde polynomial
d. Coefficient

28. In abstract algebra, _____ is an invariant which measures the homological complexity of representations of a group. It has important applications in geometric group theory, topology, and algebraic number theory.

As most (co)homological invariants, the _____ involves a choice of a 'ring of coefficients' R, with a prominent special case given by R = Z, the ring of integers.

a. Representation theory
c. Free group
b. Conjugacy class
d. Cohomological dimension

29. In mathematics, the _____ is a quotient of orders of cohomology groups of a cyclic group. It was invented by Jacques Herbrand.

If G is a finite cyclic group acting on a module A, then the cohomology groups $H^n(G,A)$ have period 2 for n≥1; in other words

$$H^n(G,A) = H^{n+2}(G,A.)$$

a. Different ideal
c. Discriminant of an algebraic number field
b. Modulus
d. Herbrand quotient

30. In mathematics, especially in elementary arithmetic, _____ is an arithmetic operation which is the inverse of multiplication.

Specifically, if c times b equals a, written:

$$c \times b = a$$

where b is not zero, then a divided by b equals c, written:

$$\frac{a}{b} = c$$

Chapter 10. Homology

For instance,

$$\frac{6}{3} = 2$$

since

$$2 \times 3 = 6.$$

In the above expression, a is called the dividend, b the divisor and c the quotient.

a. -module
b. Division
c. -equivalence
d. 2-bridge knot

31. In mathematics, a _____ is an indexed set S_i of subobjects of a given algebraic structure S, with the index i running over some index set I that is a totally ordered set, subject to the condition that if i ≤ j in I then $S_i \subseteq S_j$. The concept dual to a _____ is called a cofiltration.

Sometimes, as in a filtered algebra, there is instead the requirement that the S_i be subobjects with respect to certain operations (say, vector addition), but with respect to other operations (say, multiplication), they instead satisfy $S_i \cdot S_j \subset S_{i+j}$, where here the index set is the natural numbers; this is by analogy with a graded algebra.

a. Continuant
b. Filtration
c. Symmetric difference
d. Finitary operation

32. In the mathematical fields of category theory and abstract algebra, a _____ is a quotient object of a subobject. Subquotients are particularly important in group theory, where they are also known as sections, and in abelian categories.

a. Radical
b. Subquotient
c. Tight closure
d. Moore matrix

Chapter 11. Commutative Rings III

1. The column _____ of a matrix A is the maximal number of linearly independent columns of A. Likewise, the row _____ is the maximal number of linearly independent rows of A.

   Since the column _____ and the row _____ are always equal, they are simply called the _____ of A. More abstractly, it is the dimension of the image of A. For the proofs, see, e.g., Murase (1960), Andrea ' Wong (1960), Williams ' Cater (1968), Mackiw (1995.) It is commonly denoted by either rk(A) or _____ A.

   a. Schur complement
   b. Generalized Pauli matrices
   c. Split-complex number
   d. Rank

2. In mathematics, a _____ on a field k is a function

   $$\nu : k \to \mathbb{Z} \cup \{\infty\}$$

   satisfying the conditions

   $$\nu(x \cdot y) = \nu(x) + \nu(y)$$
   $$\nu(x + y) \geq \min\{\nu(x), \nu(y)\}$$
   $$\nu(x) = \infty \iff x = 0$$

   Note that often the trivial valuation which takes on only the values $0, \infty$ is explicitly excluded.

   To every field with _____ v we can associate the subring

   $$\mathcal{O}_k := \{x \in k \mid \nu(x) \geq 0\}$$

   of k, which is a _____ ring.

   a. Discrete valuation
   b. Going up
   c. Nilradical
   d. Commutative ring

3. In abstract algebra, a _____ is a principal ideal domain (PID) with exactly one non-zero maximal ideal.

Chapter 11. Commutative Rings III

This means a _____ is an integral domain R which satisfies any one of the following equivalent conditions:

1. R is a local principal ideal domain, and not a field.
2. R is a valuation ring with a value group isomorphic to the integers under addition.
3. R is a local Dedekind domain and not a field.
4. R is a noetherian local ring with Krull dimension one, and the maximal ideal of R is principal.
5. R is an integrally closed noetherian local ring with Krull dimension one.
6. R is a unique factorization domain with a unique irreducible element (up to multiplication with units.)
7. R is local, not a field, and every nonzero fractional ideal of R is irreducible.
8. There is some Dedekind valuation v on the field of fractions K of R, such that R={x : x in K, v(x) ≥ 0}.

Let $Z_{(2)}$={ p/q : p, q in Z, q odd }. Then the field of fractions of $Z_{(2)}$ is Q. Now, for any nonzero element r of Q, we can apply unique factorization to the numerator and denominator of r to write r as 2^kp/q, where p, q, and k are integers with p and q odd. In this case, we define v(r)=k.

a. Localization of a module
b. Localized
c. Discrete valuation ring
d. Localization of a category

4. In mathematics, a _____ is a type of algebraic structure. There is some variation among mathematicians as to exactly what properties a _____ is required to have, as described in detail below. However, commonly a _____ is defined as a set together with two binary operations (usually called addition and multiplication), where each operation combines two elements to form a third element.

a. -equivalence
b. -module
c. 2-bridge knot
d. Ring

5. In algebra (in particular in algebraic geometry or algebraic number theory), a _____ is a function on a field that provides a measure of size or multiplicity of elements of the field. They generalize to commutative algebra the notion of size inherent in consideration of the degree of a pole or multiplicity of a zero in complex analysis, the degree divisibility of a number by a prime number in number theory, and the geometrical concept of contact between two algebraic or analytic varieties in algebraic geometry.

A field with a _____ on it is called a valued field.

a. Motivic integration
b. Stable vector bundle
c. Pencil
d. Valuation

6. In abstract algebra, a _____ is an integral domain D such that for every element x of its field of fractions F, at least one of x or x^{-1} belongs to D.

Given a field F, if D is a subring of F such that either x or x^{-1} belongs to D for every x in F, then D is said to be a _____ for the field F. Since F is in this case indeed the field of fractions of D, a _____ for a field is a _____. Another way to characterize the valuation rings of a field F is that valuation rings D of F have F as their field of fractions, and their ideals are totally ordered by inclusion; or equivalently their principal ideals are totally ordered by inclusion.

a. Near-field
b. Left alternative
c. Valuation ring
d. Rupture field

7. An _____ is a group satisfying the requirement that the result of applying the group operation to two group elements does not depend on their order Abelian groups generalize the arithmetic of addition of integers; they are named after Niels Henrik Abel.

The concept of an _____ is one of the first concepts encountered in undergraduate abstract algebra, with many other basic objects, such as a module and a vector space, being its refinements.

a. Elementary abelian group
b. Algebraically compact
c. ADE classification
d. Abelian group

8. A _____ is a set G closed under a binary operation · satisfying the following 3 axioms:

- Associativity: For all a, b and c in G, (a · b) · c = a · (b · c).
- Identity element: There exists an e∈G such that for all a in G, e · a = a · e = a.
- Inverse element: For each a in G, there is an element b in G such that a · b = b · a = e, where e is an identity element.

Basic examples for groups are the integers Z with addition operation, or rational numbers without zero Q{0} with multiplication. More generally, for any ring R, the units in R form a multiplicative _____ Groups include, however, much more general structures than the above.

a. Grigorchuk group
b. Nilpotent group
c. Product of group subsets
d. Group

9. In mathematics, the _____ and length of a polynomial P with complex coefficients are measures of its 'size'.

For a polynomial P given by

$$P = a_0 + a_1 x + a_2 x^2 + \cdots + a_n x^n,$$

the _____ H(P) is defined to be the maximum of the magnitudes of its coefficients:

$$H(P) = \max_i |a_i|$$

and the length L(P) is similarly defined as the sum of the magnitudes of the coefficients:

$$L(P) = \sum_{i=0}^{n} |a_i|.$$

Chapter 11. Commutative Rings III

For a complex polynomial P of degree n, the _____ H(P), length L(P) and Mahler measure M(P) are related by the double inequalities

$$\binom{n}{\lfloor n/2 \rfloor}^{-1} H(P) \leq M(P) \leq H(P)\sqrt{n+1};$$

$$L(p) \leq 2^n M(p) \leq 2^n L(p);$$

$$H(p) \leq L(p) \leq nH(p)$$

where $\binom{n}{\lfloor n/2 \rfloor}$ is the binomial coefficient.

a. Schwartz-Bruhat function
b. Cyclotomic unit
c. Height
d. Birch and Swinnerton-Dyer conjecture

10. In mathematics, a phenomenon is sometimes said to occur _____ if, roughly speaking, it occurs on sufficiently small or arbitrarily small neighborhoods of points.

A topological space is sometimes said to exhibit a property _____ if the property is exhibited 'near' each point in one of the following different senses:

1. Each point has a neighborhood exhibiting the property;
2. Each point has a neighborhood base of sets exhibiting the property.

Sense (2) is in general stronger than sense (1), and caution must be taken to distinguish between the two senses. For example, some variation in the definition of _____ compact arises from different senses of the term _____.

- _____ compact topological spaces
- _____ connected and _____ path-connected topological spaces
- _____ Hausdorff, _____ regular, _____ normal etc...
- _____ metrizable

Given some notion of equivalence (e.g., homeomorphism, diffeomorphism, isometry) between topological spaces, two spaces are _____ equivalent if every point of the first space has a neighborhood which is equivalent to a neighborhood of the second space.

For instance, the circle and the line are very different objects.

a. Collapse
b. Locally
c. Perko pair
d. Plus construction

Chapter 11. Commutative Rings III

11. In abstract algebra, _____ is a systematic method of adding multiplicative inverses to a ring. Given a ring R and a subset S, one wants to construct some ring R* and ring homomorphism from R to R*, such that the image of S consists of units (invertible elements) in R*. Further one wants R* to be the 'best possible' or 'most general' way to do this - in the usual fashion this should be expressed by a universal property.

   a. Discrete valuation ring
   b. Localization
   c. Localization of a category
   d. Localization of a module

12. In abstract algebra, the concept of a _____ over a ring is a generalization of the notion of vector space, where instead of requiring the scalars to lie in a field, the 'scalars' may lie in an arbitrary ring. Modules also generalize the notion of abelian groups, which are modules over $\mathbb{Z}$.

   Thus, a _____, like a vector space, is an additive abelian group; a product is defined between elements of the ring and elements of the _____, and this multiplication is associative (when used with the multiplication in the ring) and distributive.

   a. Module
   b. Goodman-Nguyen-van Fraassen algebra
   c. Near-field
   d. Semigroupoid

13. In mathematics, especially in the area of abstract algebra known as ring theory, a _____ is a ring with 0 ≠ 1 such that ab = 0 implies that either a = 0 or b = 0 (the zero-product property.) That is, it is a nontrivial ring without left or right zero divisors. A commutative _____ is called an integral _____.

   a. Partially-ordered ring
   b. Subring
   c. Domain
   d. Coherent ring

14. In mathematics, _____ or factoring is the decomposition of an object ' href='/wiki/Matrix_(mathematics)'>matrix) into a product of other objects, or factors, which when multiplied together give the original. For example, the number 15 factors into primes as 3 × 5, and the polynomial $x^2 - 4$ factors as $(x - 2)(x + 2)$. In all cases, a product of simpler objects is obtained.

   a. -module
   b. -equivalence
   c. 2-bridge knot
   d. Factorization

15. In mathematics, a _____ is, roughly speaking, a commutative ring in which every element, with special exceptions, can be uniquely written as a product of prime elements, analogous to the fundamental theorem of arithmetic for the integers. Unique factorization domains are sometimes called factorial rings, following the terminology of Bourbaki.

   Note that unique factorization domains appear in the following chain of class inclusions:

   - Commutative rings >⊃ integral domains >⊃ unique factorization domains >⊃ principal ideal domains >⊃ Euclidean domains >⊃ fields

   a. Isomorphism class
   b. Absorption law
   c. Unit ring
   d. Unique factorization domain

16. In mathematics, in the realm of ring theory, a commutative ring with identity is said to be a Hilbert ring or a _____ if every prime ideal of the ring is an intersection of maximal ideals.

Chapter 11. Commutative Rings III

In a commutative unital ring, every radical ideal is an intersection of prime ideals, and hence, an equivalent criterion for a ring to be Hilbert is that every radical ideal is an intersection of maximal ideals.

The famous Nullstellensatz of algebraic geometry translates to the statement that the polynomial ring in finitely many variables over a field is a Hilbert ring.

a. Minimal prime
b. Quasi-homogeneous polynomial
c. Laurent polynomial
d. Jacobson ring

17. In linear algebra, a _____ is a set of vectors that, in a linear combination, can represent every vector in a given vector space or free module, and such that no element of the set can be represented as a linear combination of the others. In other words, a _____ is a linearly independent spanning set.

a. Minor
b. Supergroup
c. Chirality
d. Basis

18. In ring theory, a branch of abstract algebra, an _____ is a special subset of a ring. The _____ concept generalizes in an appropriate way some important properties of integers like 'even number' or 'multiple of 3'.

For instance, in rings one studies prime ideals instead of prime numbers, one defines coprime ideals as a generalization of coprime numbers, and one can prove a generalized Chinese remainder theorem about ideals.

a. Ideal
b. ADE classification
c. Augmentation ideal
d. AKS primality test

19. In commutative algebra, the notions of an element _____ over a ring, and of an _____ extension of rings, are a generalization of the notions in field theory of an element being algebraic over a field, and of an algebraic extension of fields.

The special case of greatest interest in number theory is that of complex numbers _____ over the ring of integers Z.

a. Associated prime
b. Integral
c. Extension and contraction of ideals
d. Integral domain

20. In mathematics, more specifically in ring theory, a _____ or extension ring is a ring R with a subring S. We write R/S and say R is a _____ of S

Given an extension R/S of commutative rings and a prime ideal P of R, it follows that the intersection, say p, of P with S is a prime ideal of S. In this case we say that P lies over p. The situation is more complicated when R is not commutative.

- A field extension is a special case of _____.

a. Fox derivative
b. Semiprimitive ring
c. Birational invariant
d. Ring extension

21. In mathematics, an _____ is a complex number that is a root of a non-zero polynomial in one variable with rational (or equivalently, integer) coefficients. Numbers such as pi that are not algebraic are said to be transcendental, and are infinitely more numerous within the complex number field.

- The rational numbers, those expressed as the ratio of two whole numbers b and a, a not equal to zero, satisfy the above definition because x = − b / a is derived from (and satisfies) ax + b = 0. (In general, a or b can be negative, as can x.)

- Some irrational numbers are algebraic and some are not:

    - The numbers $\sqrt{2}$ and $\sqrt[3]{3}/2$ are algebraic since they are the roots of $x^2 - 2 = 0$ and $8x^3 - 3 = 0$, respectively.

    - The golden ratio φ is algebraic since it is a root of the polynomial $x^2 - x - 1 = 0$.

    - The numbers π and e are not algebraic numbers ; hence they are transcendental.

- The constructible numbers (those that, starting with a unit, can be constructed with straightedge and compass, e.g. the square root of 2) are algebraic.

- The quadratic surds (roots of a quadratic equation $ax^2 + bx + c = 0$ with integer coefficients a, b, and c) are algebraic numbers. Thus those complex numbers derived from $ax^2 + bx + c = 0$ -- those corresponding to the case when the exponent n = 2 -- are called quadratic numbers.

a. Universal algebra
b. Algebraic number
c. External
d. Unit ring

22. In mathematics, an _____ F is a finite (and hence algebraic) field extension of the field of rational numbers Q. Thus F is a field that contains Q and has finite dimension when considered as a vector space over Q.

The study of algebraic number fields, and, more generally, of algebraic extensions of the field of rational numbers, is the central topic of algebraic number theory.

Suppose F is a field extension of the field of rational numbers Q of finite degree n.

a. Algebraic number field
b. Algebraic integer
c. Adele ring
d. Additive polynomial

23. In abstract algebra, a _____ is an algebraic structure with notions of addition, subtraction, multiplication and division, satisfying certain axioms. The most commonly used fields are the _____ of real numbers, the _____ of complex numbers, and the _____ of rational numbers, but there are also finite fields, fields of functions, various algebraic number fields, p-adic fields, and so forth.

Any _____ may be used as the scalars for a vector space, which is the standard general context for linear algebra.

a. Tensor product of fields
c. Separable
b. Generic polynomial
d. Field

24. The _____ are natural numbers including 0 ' href='/wiki/0_(number)'>0, 1, 2, 3, ...) and their negatives (0, −1, −2, −3, ...). They are numbers that can be written without a fractional or decimal component, and fall within the set {...

a. Abelian P-root group
c. ADE classification
b. AKS primality test
d. Integers

25. In mathematics, more specifically in abstract algebra, the concept of _____ has two meanings, one for groups and one for rings.

A commutative ring R contained in a ring S is said to be _____ in S if every element of the integral closure of R in S is also in R. That is, every monic polynomial with coefficients in R has all of its roots in R.

a. ADE classification
c. Ordered field
b. Integrally closed
d. Ordered ring

26. In mathematics, the _____ of a ring R, often denoted char(R), is defined to be the smallest number of times one must add the ring's multiplicative identity element (1) to itself to get the additive identity element (0); the ring is said to have _____ zero if this repeated sum never reaches the additive identity. That is, char(R) is the smallest positive number n such that

$$\underbrace{1 + \cdots + 1}_{n \text{ summands}} = 0$$

if such a number n exists, and 0 otherwise. The _____ may also be taken to be the exponent of the ring's additive group, that is, the smallest positive n such that

$$\underbrace{a + \cdots + a}_{n \text{ summands}} = 0$$

for every element a of the ring (again, if n exists; otherwise zero.)

a. Hereditary
c. Coherent ring
b. Free ideal ring
d. Characteristic

27. In commutative algebra, a branch of mathematics, _____ and going down are terms which refer to certain properties of chains of prime ideals in integral extensions.

The phrase _____ refers to the case when a chain can be extended by 'upward inclusion', while going down refers to the case when a chain can be extended by 'downward inclusion'.

The major results are the Cohen-Seidenberg theorems, which were proved by Irving S. Cohen and Abraham Seidenberg.

- a. Divided power structure
- b. Krull dimension
- c. Hilbert polynomial
- d. Going up

28. In mathematics, a _____ is an algebraic structure whose main use is in studying geometric objects such as Lie groups and differentiable manifolds. Lie algebras were introduced to study the concept of infinitesimal transformations. The term '_____') was introduced by Hermann Weyl in the 1930s.

- a. Maximal torus
- b. Weyl group
- c. Lorentz group
- d. Lie algebra

29. In algebra, the _____ of a commutative ring is a nilpotent ideal, which is as large as possible. In the non-commutative ring case, more care is needed resulting in several related radicals.

The _____ of a commutative ring is the set of all nilpotent elements in the ring, or equivalently the radical of the zero ideal.

- a. Top
- b. Hilbert polynomial
- c. Noether normalization lemma
- d. Nilradical

30. In mathematics, a _____ is an algebraic number field K of degree two over Q. It is easy to show that the map d↦Q (√d) is a bijection from the set of all square-free integers d≠0,1 to the set of all quadratic fields. If d > 0 the corresponding _____ is called a real _____, and for d < 0 an imaginary _____ or complex _____, corresponding to whether its archimedean embeddings are real or complex.

Quadratic fields are a basic object of study and class of examples in algebraic number theory.

- a. Hasse norm theorem
- b. Fundamental unit
- c. Quadratic field
- d. Herbrand quotient

31. In linear algebra, functional analysis and related areas of mathematics, a _____ is a function that assigns a strictly positive length or size to all vectors in a vector space, other than the zero vector. A seminorm (or pseudonorm), on the other hand, is allowed to assign zero length to some non-zero vectors.

A simple example is the 2-dimensional Euclidean space R^2 equipped with the Euclidean _____.

- a. Quasinorm
- b. -module
- c. -equivalence
- d. Norm

32. In linear algebra, the _____ of an n-by-n square matrix A is defined to be the sum of the elements on the main diagonal (the diagonal from the upper left to the lower right) of A, i.e.,

Chapter 11. Commutative Rings III

$$\text{tr}(A) = a_{11} + a_{22} + \cdots + a_{nn} = \sum_{i=1}^{n} a_{ii}$$

where a_{ij} represents the entry on the ith row and jth column of A. Equivalently, the _____ of a matrix is the sum of its eigenvalues, making it an invariant with respect to a change of basis. This characterization can be used to define the _____ for a linear operator in general.

Note that the _____ is only defined for a square matrix (i.e. n×n.)

a. Coefficient matrix
c. Dot product
b. Defective matrix
d. Trace

33. In number theory, a _____ is a number field obtained by adjoining a complex root of unity to Q, the field of rational numbers. The n-th _____ $Q(\zeta_n)$ (with n > 2) is obtained by adjoining a primitive n-th root of unity ζ_n to the rational numbers.

The cyclotomic fields played a crucial role in the development of modern algebra and number theory because of their relation with Fermat's last theorem.

a. Discriminant of an algebraic number field
c. Compatible system of â„"-adic representations
b. S-units
d. Cyclotomic field

34. In mathematics, in particular commutative algebra, the idea of _____ is introduced in the context of Dedekind domains. In general commutative rings there is no guarantee that one can divide an ideal I by another one J that is non-zero, and get a satisfactory inverse to multiplication of ideals. But that is possible under special circumstances that play an important part in algebraic number theory.

a. Fractional ideal
c. Principal ideal
b. Jacobson radical
d. Primitive ideal

35. Let S be a set with a binary operation * . If e is an identity element of (S, *) and a * b = e, then a is called a _____ of b and b is called a right inverse of a. If an element x is both a _____ and a right inverse of y, then x is called a two-sided inverse, or simply an inverse, of y.

a. -equivalence
c. 2-bridge knot
b. -module
d. Left inverse

36. In mathematics, especially in the area of abstract algebra known as module theory, a ring R is called _____ if all submodules of projective modules over R are again projective. If this is required only for finitely generated submodules, it is called semihereditary.

For a noncommutative ring R, the terms left (semi-)_____ submodules of projective left R-modules are projective) and right (semi-)_____ are sometimes used.

a. Subring test
c. Domain
b. Hereditary
d. GCD domain

37. In mathematics, the _____ construction in abstract algebra constructs an abelian group from a commutative monoid in the best possible way. It takes its name from the more general construction in category theory, introduced by Alexander Grothendieck in his fundamental work of the mid-1950s that resulted in the development of K-theory. The _____ is denoted by K or K_0.

a. Coimage
c. Power set
b. Restriction of scalars
d. Grothendieck group

38. In mathematics, the _____ of a ringed space X, denoted by $\mathrm{Pic}(X)$, is the group of isomorphism classes of invertible sheaves on X, with the group operation being tensor product. This construction is a global version of the construction of the divisor class group, or ideal class group, and is much used in algebraic geometry, and the theory of complex manifolds.

Alternatively, the _____ can be defined as the sheaf cohomology group

$$H^1(X, \mathcal{O}_X^*).$$

For integral schemes the _____ can be shown to be isomorphic to the class group of Cartier divisors.

a. Normal crossing divisor
c. Lefschetz pencil
b. Linear system of divisors
d. Picard group

39. In mathematics, the _____ of a vector space V is the cardinality (i.e. the number of vectors) of a basis of V. It is sometimes called Hamel _____ or algebraic _____ to distinguish it from other types of _____. All bases of a vector space have equal cardinality and so the _____ of a vector space is uniquely defined. The _____ of the vector space V over the field F can be written as $\dim_F(V)$ or as [V : F], read '_____ of V over F'.

a. Dual basis
c. Partial trace
b. Dimension
d. Cofactor

40. In ring theory and homological algebra, the _____ of a ring A denoted gl dim A, is a non-negative integer or infinity which is a homological invariant of the ring. It is defined to be the supremum of the set of projective dimensions of all A-modules. _____ is an important technical notion in the dimension theory of Noetherian rings.

a. Global dimension
c. Regular ring
b. Free ideal ring
d. GCD domain

41. In geometry, a _____ is a subset of n-dimensional space that is congruent to a Euclidean space of lower dimension. The flats in two-dimensional space are points and lines, and the flats in three-dimensional space are points, lines, and planes. In n-dimensional space, there are flats of every dimension from 0 to n - 1.

a. -module
c. Flat
b. -equivalence
d. Similarity

42. In mathematics, particularly in abstract algebra and homological algebra, a _____ is a sequence which is used to describe the structure of a module.

Chapter 11. Commutative Rings III

If the modules involved in the sequence have a property P then one speaks of a P _____ : for example, a flat _____, a free _____, an injective _____, a projective _____ and so on.

Given a module M over a ring R, a _____ of M is an exact sequence (possibly infinite) of modules

$$\cdots \to E_n \to \cdots \to E_2 \to E_1 \to E_0 \to M \to 0,$$

with all the E_i modules over R. The _____ is said to be finite if the sequence of E_i is zero from some point onwards.

a. Resolution
b. Projective representation
c. Homological algebra
d. Hodge structure

43. In mathematics, the _____ is a basic construction in commutative algebra. If R is a commutative ring and m is a maximal ideal, then the _____ is the quotient ring k = R/m, which is a field. Frequently, R is a local ring and m is then its unique maximal ideal.
    a. Deformation theory
    b. Residue field
    c. Generic point
    d. Direction cosines

44. In mathematics, a _____ is a subset of a ring which shares many important properties of a prime number in the ring of integers Prime ideals in order theory are treated in the article on ideals in order theory.
    a. Prime ideal
    b. Radical of an ideal
    c. Principal ideal
    d. Radical of an ring

45. In commutative algebra, the _____ of a ring R is defined to be the number of strict inclusions in a maximal chain of prime ideals. The _____ need not be finite.

A field (more generally a finite dimensional vector space over a field) has the _____ 0, and a PID that is not a field (or more generally a Dedekind domain that is not a field) has the _____ 1.

a. Polynomial ring
b. Total quotient ring
c. Dedekind domain
d. Krull dimension

46. In ring theory, a branch of abstract algebra, a _____ is an ideal I in a ring R that is generated by a single element a of R.

More specifically:

- a left _____ of R is a subset of R of the form Ra := {ra : r in R};
- a right _____ is a subset of the form aR := {ar : r in R};
- a two-sided _____ is a subset of the form RaR := {$r_1 a s_1$ + ... + $r_n a s_n$: $r_1, s_1, ..., r_n, s_n$ in R}.

If R is a commutative ring, then the above three notions are all the same. In that case, it is common to write the ideal generated by a as (a.)

Not all ideals are principal.

a. Radical of an ring
b. Radical of an ideal
c. Primitive ideal
d. Principal ideal

47. In mathematics, the _____ of class field theory, a branch of algebraic number theory, is the statement that for any algebraic number field K and any ideal I of the ring of integers of K, if L is the Hilbert class field of K, then

IO_L

is a principal ideal $αO_L$, for O_L the ring of integers of L and some element α in it. In other terms, extending ideals gives a mapping on the class group of K, to the class group of L, which sends all ideal classes to the class of a principal ideal. The phenomenon has also been called principalization, or sometimes capitulation.

a. Splitting of prime ideals in Galois extensions
b. Discriminant of an algebraic number field
c. Principal ideal theorem
d. Hasse principle

48. In commutative algebra, a _____ is a Noetherian local ring having the property that the minimal number of generators of its maximal ideal is exactly the same as its Krull dimension. The minimal number of generators of the maximal ideal is always bounded below by the Krull dimension. In symbols, let A be a local ring with maximal ideal m, and suppose that m is generated by $a_1, ..., a_n$.

a. Direction cosines
b. Regular local ring
c. Rational map
d. Flat topology

49. In commutative algebra, if R is a commutative ring and M an R-module, an element r in R is called M-regular if r is not a zerodivisor on M, and M/rM is nonzero. An R-_____ on M is a d-tuple

$r_1, ..., r_d$ in R

such that for each i ≤ d, r_i is M_{i-1}-regular, where M_{i-1} is the quotient R-module

$M/(r_1, ..., r_{i-1})M$.

Such a sequence is also called an M-sequence.

a. Going up
b. Local parameter
c. Regular sequence
d. Commutative ring

Chapter 11. Commutative Rings III

50. In mathematics, _____ are devices that make it possible to employ much of the analytical machinery of power series in settings that do not have natural notions of convergence. They are also useful, especially in combinatorics, for providing compact representations of sequences and multisets, and for finding closed formulas for recursively defined sequences; this is known as the method of generating functions.

A _____ can be loosely thought of as a polynomial with infinitely many terms.

   a. Matrix
   c. Multiplicative group
   b. Cokernel
   d. Formal power series

51. In abstract algebra, a _____ i.e., can be generated by a single element. More generally, a principal ring is a nonzero commutative ring whose ideals are principal, although some authors (e.g., Bourbaki) refers to Principal ideal domains as principal rings. The distinction being that a principal ideal ring may have zero divisors whereas a _____ cannot.
   a. Discrete valuation
   c. Nilradical
   b. Minimal prime
   d. Principal ideal domain

ANSWER KEY

Chapter 1
1. d 2. b 3. d 4. d 5. a 6. d 7. d 8. d 9. a 10. d
11. d 12. d 13. a 14. d 15. d 16. d 17. d 18. d 19. c 20. d
21. d 22. d 23. d 24. a 25. d 26. a 27. d 28. b 29. d 30. d
31. d 32. d

Chapter 2
1. b 2. a 3. d 4. d 5. d 6. a 7. a 8. c 9. a 10. c
11. d 12. d 13. b 14. b 15. d 16. d 17. d 18. d 19. d 20. d
21. b 22. a 23. c 24. d 25. d 26. a 27. d 28. c 29. d 30. a
31. d 32. a 33. c 34. b 35. d 36. b 37. c 38. d 39. d 40. c
41. d 42. a 43. c 44. c 45. a 46. b 47. d 48. d 49. a 50. a

Chapter 3
1. d 2. c 3. a 4. b 5. d 6. d 7. b 8. b 9. d 10. b
11. d 12. a 13. d 14. d 15. c 16. c 17. a 18. d 19. d 20. a
21. c 22. a 23. c 24. d 25. d 26. d 27. b 28. b 29. a 30. a
31. d 32. a 33. a 34. a 35. d 36. d 37. c 38. d 39. a 40. d
41. d 42. d 43. d 44. d 45. c 46. b 47. a 48. a 49. d 50. d
51. d 52. d 53. d 54. d 55. a 56. d 57. c 58. d 59. d 60. d
61. d 62. d 63. d 64. d 65. b 66. d 67. d

Chapter 4
1. d 2. a 3. d 4. b 5. d 6. d 7. d 8. d 9. b 10. a
11. c 12. d 13. a 14. c 15. d 16. d 17. d 18. b 19. c 20. c
21. c 22. b 23. d 24. a 25. a 26. b 27. b

Chapter 5
1. a 2. d 3. b 4. b 5. c 6. d 7. d 8. a 9. b 10. a
11. b 12. a 13. b 14. d 15. d 16. d 17. d 18. d 19. d 20. d
21. c 22. a 23. b 24. a 25. b 26. a 27. d 28. d 29. d 30. d
31. c 32. a 33. b 34. d 35. b 36. c

Chapter 6
1. a 2. b 3. b 4. b 5. d 6. d 7. c 8. d 9. a 10. b
11. d 12. c 13. b 14. b 15. c 16. a 17. c 18. a 19. c 20. a
21. d 22. a 23. b 24. a 25. c 26. c 27. c 28. a 29. d 30. c
31. d 32. b 33. d 34. d 35. d 36. d 37. d 38. d 39. c 40. d
41. d 42. b 43. b 44. d 45. d 46. b 47. d 48. a 49. b 50. d
51. d 52. d 53. d 54. d 55. d 56. d 57. d 58. c 59. b

ANSWER KEY

Chapter 7

1. d	2. d	3. d	4. c	5. d	6. d	7. d	8. c	9. c	10. d
11. d	12. b	13. b	14. d	15. a	16. c	17. d	18. d	19. d	20. d
21. d	22. d	23. a	24. d	25. d	26. d	27. a	28. d	29. d	30. b
31. c	32. a	33. c	34. d	35. a	36. a	37. d	38. d	39. b	40. c
41. d	42. b	43. b	44. d	45. b	46. d	47. c			

Chapter 8

1. d	2. d	3. d	4. a	5. d	6. d	7. a	8. d	9. d	10. a
11. d	12. d	13. a	14. d	15. b	16. a	17. a	18. d	19. d	20. b
21. d	22. d	23. d	24. d	25. d	26. a	27. d	28. b	29. c	30. b
31. b	32. c	33. b	34. d	35. d	36. a	37. d	38. d	39. a	40. d
41. a	42. c	43. c	44. a	45. c	46. d	47. b	48. d	49. d	50. d
51. d	52. c	53. a	54. d	55. d	56. d	57. d	58. c	59. b	60. d
61. b	62. c	63. a	64. d	65. c	66. d	67. b	68. d	69. d	70. c
71. d	72. d								

Chapter 9

1. d	2. d	3. c	4. a	5. a	6. d	7. d	8. c	9. d	10. b
11. c	12. d	13. c	14. c	15. d	16. d	17. b	18. d	19. d	20. d
21. b	22. d	23. d	24. d	25. c	26. d	27. a	28. a	29. b	30. d
31. d	32. d	33. c	34. a	35. d	36. d	37. c	38. d	39. d	40. d
41. d	42. d	43. d	44. d	45. d	46. b	47. c	48. d	49. d	50. a
51. a	52. a	53. c	54. d	55. d	56. a	57. c	58. b	59. c	60. c
61. c	62. b	63. c	64. b	65. b	66. a	67. d	68. d	69. a	70. d
71. d	72. d	73. d	74. c	75. c	76. b	77. d	78. b	79. a	80. c
81. c	82. a	83. d							

Chapter 10

1. d	2. d	3. d	4. d	5. d	6. b	7. d	8. d	9. a	10. d
11. a	12. c	13. b	14. a	15. a	16. d	17. d	18. d	19. d	20. b
21. c	22. b	23. b	24. b	25. d	26. d	27. d	28. d	29. d	30. b
31. b	32. b								

Chapter 11

1. d	2. a	3. c	4. d	5. d	6. c	7. d	8. d	9. c	10. b
11. b	12. a	13. c	14. d	15. d	16. d	17. d	18. a	19. b	20. d
21. b	22. a	23. d	24. d	25. b	26. d	27. d	28. d	29. d	30. c
31. d	32. d	33. d	34. a	35. d	36. b	37. d	38. d	39. b	40. a
41. c	42. a	43. b	44. a	45. d	46. d	47. c	48. b	49. c	50. d
51. d									

www.ingramcontent.com/pod-product-compliance
Lightning Source LLC
Chambersburg PA
CBHW082040230426

43670CB00016B/2725